Herbert Puchta & Jeff Stranks

English in Mind

Second edition

Workbook 2

CAMBRIDGE
UNIVERSITY PRESS

Welcome section

1 Present simple vs. present continuous

Write the verbs in the correct form of the present simple or present continuous.

Mum: Where's Alex?

Molly: He's upstairs. He [1] *is having* (have) a shower.

Mum: A shower? But it's 7 o'clock in the evening. Alex always [2] _____ (have) a shower in the morning.

Molly: That's right. But this evening is different. He [3] _____ (get) ready to go out. So he [4] _____ (wash) his hair, too.

Mum: What? He never [5] _____ (wash) his hair. Well, not on Thursday, anyway.

Molly: Yes, that's true.

Mum: Just a minute. I can hear a strange noise.

Molly: Yes, that's Alex. He [6] _____ (sing) in the shower. It's because he's very happy. He asked Ellie to go to the cinema with him, and she said 'Yes'. He [7] _____ (like) her – a lot!

2 Hobbies and interests

Circle seven -ing words used for hobbies and interests in the wordsearch (↓ → ↑).

E	P	L	A	Y	I	N	G	R	I
N	R	I	N	N	O	N	O	U	N
R	E	S	W	I	M	M	I	N	G
E	L	T	I	R	R	A	N	I	N
A	Y	E	M	B	U	T	G	N	I
D	A	N	C	I	N	G	L	G	T
I	I	I	I	G	N	R	O	S	N
N	E	N	O	T	I	N	G	I	I
G	N	G	S	A	N	T	N	N	A
P	L	A	I	N	G	O	I	N	P

3 Jobs

Complete the sentences with the words from the box.

architect ~~dentist~~ doctor teacher flight attendant lawyer pilot firefighter shop assistant vet

1 If you've got toothache, why don't you go and see a _____ *dentist* _____ ?

2 The plane landed safely, because the _____ knew exactly what to do.

3 When I bought these shoes, the _____ told me the wrong price.

4 My mum helped put out the big fire last night, she's a _____ .

5 When my friend was in trouble with the police, his dad had to get a _____ to help.

6 Our dog got ill and we had to call the _____ .

7 A very famous _____ designed that house.

8 While we were flying to Madrid, the _____ dropped some food on my dad's head!

9 My sister's a History _____ in a school in north London.

10 I had a terrible cold, but the _____ gave me some medicine, and now I'm better.

B

1 Much/many

Complete the sentences with *much* or *many*.

1 I haven't got _____many_____ friends at school.

2 Our teacher didn't give us _____ homework today.

3 How _____ bedrooms are there in your house?

4 There aren't _____ good places to go in this town.

5 She works really hard, but she doesn't earn _____ money.

6 How _____ food is there in the fridge?

2 Some/any

Look at the picture and then write sentences.

1 *There are some eggs.*

2 _____

3 _____

4 _____

5 _____

6 _____

7 _____

8 _____

3 Comparative and superlative adjectives

Underline the correct word in each sentence.

1 Lucy's *tall* / *tallest* but I'm *tall* / *taller* than her.

2 That's the *smallest* / *most small* cat I've ever seen.

3 Do you think Lindsay Lohan is a *best* / *better* actress than Kirsten Dunst?

4 This is the *most* / *more* interesting book I've ever read.

5 Ruby got the *higher* / *highest* marks in the test.

6 Which city is *bigger* / *biggest* – London or New York?

7 I love this game. It's the *better* / *best* one I've got.

8 We've got exams tomorrow. There's nothing *worse* / *worst* than that!

4 Multi-word verbs

Complete the sentences with *off/up/ out*.

1 If you don't know what it means, look it ____up____ in a dictionary!

2 I can't do this exercise! I'm going to give _____ !

3 Hey Jenny. This new game is brilliant! Check it _____ !

4 I got home really late. My parents told me _____ the next morning.

5 This maths homework is really difficult, but I'm sure I can work _____ the answer.

6 I didn't like running, so I decided to take _____ swimming instead.

C

1 Will/won't

Look at the pictures and complete the sentences.

Grace — go to the cinema

1 Grace thinks she
   <u>'ll go to the cinema</u>
   on Saturday.

Harry — rain tomorrow

2 Harry thinks it
   _____ .

go swimming — Sophie

3 Sophie
   _____
   this evening.

go to Italy — Jack — Charlotte

4 Jack and Charlotte probably
   _____ this
   year.

2 Adverbs

Underline the correct options.

1 He's a really *good/well* guitar player.
2 She plays the piano very *good/well*.
3 He's smiling – I think he's *happy/happily*.
4 Sorry, I don't understand – you're talking very *quick/quickly*.
5 Please be *quiet/quietly*! You're behaving very *bad/badly*!
6 I'm really *bad/badly* at Physics at school.
7 Drive *careful/carefully* – this road's very dangerous.
8 Tell me what you think. And tell me *honest/honestly*, OK?

3 be going to

Look at the pictures and complete the sentences.

 Evie
 Mike
 Alice
 Chloë & Alfie

1 Evie's <u>going to watch</u> a DVD.
2 Mike _____ a book.
3 Alice _____ for a walk.
4 Chloë and Alfie _____ tennis.

4 Future time expressions

Put the words in the correct order to make future time expressions. Then complete the sentences with the expressions.

~~day next the~~   *the next day*
tomorrow the after day   month next   two time in years'
week the next after   time hours' two in

1 The museum was closed on Sunday, so we went back
   <u>the next day</u> . (= on Monday)
2 It's 2012 now, and the next World Cup is _____ .
   (= in 2014)
3 It's May. My birthday is _____ . (= in June)
4 It's Monday. The big match is _____ .
   (= on Wednesday)
5 It's 8 o'clock. I have to be home _____ .
   (= at 10 o'clock)
6 It's 2 December. The school holidays start
   _____ . (= on 15 December)

D

1 First conditional

Put the words in the correct order to make sentences.

1 if / to the beach tomorrow / rain / We'll / doesn't / go / it

We'll go to the beach tomorrow if it doesn't rain.

2 money / I'll / if / my parents / give me / buy / for my birthday / a bike

....

3 we / won't / If / we / the game / don't / play / win / well

....

4 you / you / won't / pass / music / If / all day / listen to / your exams

....

2 Adjectives for feelings and opinions

Put the letters in brackets in the correct order to make adjectives to complete the sentences.

1 I don't like her new dress – I think it's really ....*ugly*........ (glyu)

2 He's bought an MP4 player – it's so .... ! (loco)

3 I loved the book – it was just .... (tcasanfti)

4 The film was so .... that I fell asleep after 20 minutes! (luld)

3 Personality adjectives

Use words from the wordsnake to complete each sentence.

relaxedlazyunkindfriendlyhonestmiserabledisorganisedpolite

1 Angela's very upset – Julia said a very ....*unkind*.... thing to her.

2 Her cat died yesterday so she's very .... today.

3 Frances held the door open for the old lady – she's very ....

4 I'm not a nervous person, I'm the opposite, I'm very .... !

5 Everyone likes her because she's so ....

6 I can never find anything on my desk – I'm very .... !

7 I'm not going to do anything at all today – I'm going to be really ....

8 That money isn't yours – be .... and give it back.

4 Present perfect with *ever/never*

Complete the conversation. Use the present perfect and the words in brackets.

Sarah: Hi Angus! How's your holiday?

Angus: Fantastic. London is the best city I [1] ....*'ve ever visited*.... (ever/visit). And the hotel is great too – I [2] .... (never/sleep) in such a comfortable bed!

Sarah: [3] .... you .... (ever/be) to London before, Angus?

Angus: No. In fact, I [4] .... (never/be) to England before. But I love it here. Everything's brilliant – but it's a bit expensive. Dad's a bit shocked – he [5] .... (never/spend) so much in three days before! And tonight we're going to the theatre, and then to a Japanese restaurant.

Sarah: Japanese? Oh right. [6] .... you .... (ever/eat) Japanese food?

Angus: Yes, lots of times. It's delicious.

Sarah: OK. Well, I [7] .... (never/try) it, but I believe you! OK, have a good time tonight Angus.

Angus: Thanks – I will! Bye Sarah.

1 Great idea!

1 Remember and check

a Match the words in the columns. Then check with the text on page 12 of the Student's Book.

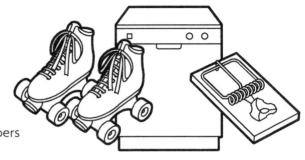

1	car driver	ice skates	dishwasher
2	rubber	window	chewing gum
3	mice	produce toys	windscreen wipers
4	after lunch	supply of potatoes	roller skates
5	summer	mountain of dishes	mouse trap

b Complete the sentences with words from Exercise 1a. Check with the text on page 12 of the Student's Book.

1 A lady from Illinois invented the
   _____dishwasher_____ .

2 Thomas Adams wanted to produce rubber.
   He invented _____ .

3 One summer day an unknown Dutchman had
   the idea for _____ .

4 Mary Anderson invented _____
   and saved the lives of many drivers.

5 James Henry Atkinson noticed mice in his
   house. He invented the _____ .

2 Grammar

✱ Past continuous

a Complete the sentences with the past continuous form of the verbs in brackets.

1 I _was making_ (make) my dog his dinner when
   you called.

2 My grandmother _____ (dance)
   to a Michael Jackson CD when I arrived.

3 The cats _____ (sit) on top of
   the piano, so I couldn't play.

4 I _____ (draw) a picture of the
   teacher on the board when he came into
   the room.

5 We _____ (laugh) loudly, so we
   didn't hear the bell.

6 Mum and Dad _____ (kiss) when
   we opened the door.

7 Nigel _____ (try) to do his
   homework on the bus.

b Look at pictures 1 and 2. Write sentences in the negative form of the past continuous. Use the verbs in the box.

cook	sleep	read	eat	have a shower
~~watch~~				

Last night at 10.00 pm …

1 my Uncle James was in the living room, but
   he _wasn't watching_ TV.

2 my parents were in the kitchen, but they
   _____ .

3 my sister, Jenny, was in the library, but she
   _____ .

4 my brother, Mike, was in the bathroom, but
   he _____ .

5 I was in bed, but I _____ .

6 my grandparents were in the dining room,
   but they _____ .

c Write questions and short answers. Use the pictures below and the words in brackets.

1 my Uncle James / read a newspaper?
Was my Uncle James reading a newspaper?
Yes, he was.

2 Jenny / read a book? (eat a sandwich)
Was Jenny reading a book?
No, she wasn't. She was _____
_____ .

3 Mike / look out of the window?
_____ ?
_____ .

4 my parents / cook dinner? (talk)
_____ ?
_____ .

5 I / watch TV? _____ ?
_____ .

6 my grandparents / eat dinner? (sleep)
_____ ?
_____ .

d Write the questions. Use the past continuous form of the verbs in brackets.

1 I phoned you on Sunday night, but there was no answer. What *were you doing*? (you / do)

2 I saw you in the Game Centre yesterday. What _____ ? (you / play)

3 I saw your mum and dad with lots of bags. Where _____ ? (they / go)

4 You put the phone down very quickly when I came in! Who _____ to? (you / talk)

5 I thought John didn't like Maria! Why _____ hands with her? (he / hold)

6 I saw your sister outside the cinema last night. Who _____ for? (she / wait)

(2)

3 # Vocabulary

✱ *get*

a Complete the sentences with the correct form of *get* and the words in the box.

confused   home   angry   presents   wet   dry

1 It was my brother's birthday last week. He .*got*. lots of *presents* .

2 Sometimes my parents _____
_____ when I don't tidy my
bedroom. _____

3 Tim didn't understand the maths exercise: he _____ very _____ .

4 I went for a walk on Sunday, but it started raining and I _____ very _____ .

5 Our plane was late and we _____
_____ at 1 am.

6 You're very wet. Come inside the house and _____ _____ .

b **Vocabulary bank** Complete the sentences with the correct form of *get* and the words in the box.

together   a chance   ~~hungry~~   sick
a lot of pleasure   a phone call

1 When I _____*get hungry*_____ I eat an apple.

2 When I _____ with my friends, we often hang out in a shopping mall.

3 My sister _____ from writing her diary.

4 The last time I _____
_____ was my 10th birthday. I ate far too much cake!

5 I hope one day I _____
_____ to learn how to scuba dive.

6 Last night I _____
_____ from my English teacher. She told me not to forget my homework!

4 Grammar

✱ Past continuous vs. past simple; *when* and *while*

a **Complete the sentences. Use the past simple or past continuous form of the verbs in brackets.**

1 While the teacher _was writing_ (write) on the board, Toby _fell_ (fall) asleep.

2 Kelly _____ (have) a shower when her mobile phone _____ (ring).

3 While Lauren _____ (watch) TV, her dog _____ (eat) her dinner.

4 Somebody _____ (steal) Dave's clothes while he _____ (swim) in the sea.

5 Jonathan's wig _____ (fall) off while he _____ (play) football.

6 While Erica _____ (sunbathe) in the garden, the cat _____ (jump) on her head.

b **Join the sentences in two different ways. Use *when* and *while*.**

1 I fell. I was playing basketball.

I fell while I was playing basketball.

I was playing basketball when I fell.

2 We were listening to music. The lights went off.

----

3 I lost my keys. I was running on the beach.

----

4 Somebody stole my bag. I was talking to my friend.

----

5 Danny called. You were taking the dog for a walk.

----

6 I was getting ready for the beach. It started to rain.

----

c **Complete the sentences with your own ideas, or use the pictures to help you.**

1 While I was using my computer at the weekend, *I sent an email to one of my friends.*

2 When I came into the classroom today,

--------------------------------.

3 While I was eating dinner last night,

--------------------------------.

4 While I was cleaning my teeth last night,

--------------------------------.

5 While I was doing my homework last night,

--------------------------------.

6 When I left the house this morning,

--------------------------------.

5 Pronunciation

✱ *was* and *were*

▶ CD3 T8 Listen and <u>underline</u> the main stress. Then listen again and repeat.

1 A: I was <u>waiting</u> for you.

   B: <u>No</u>, you <u>weren't</u>! You were <u>going</u> <u>without</u> me.

2 A: You <u>weren't</u> <u>crying</u>.

   B: Yes, I <u>was</u>!

3 A: She was sleeping.

   B: No, she wasn't! She was reading.

4 A: They were kissing.

   B: No, they weren't. They were dancing.

5 A: We were doing our homework.

   B: No, you weren't. You were playing games.

6 A: I wasn't writing a letter.

   B: Yes, you were!

6 Culture in mind

Complete the summary about the history of listening to music. Use the words in the box. Then check with the text on page 16 of the Student's Book.

> popular   records   ~~bought~~   recordings
> paper rolls   radio   invented
> steel needle   wax cylinders   disks

In the late ninetenth and early twentieth centuries, many families *bought* player pianos. These pianos played music programmed on perforated ¹ _____ , but you could also play them like a 'normal' piano. When the ² _____ (the wireless) became ³ _____ , player pianos began to disappear.

The first phonographs appeared more or less around the beginning of the twentieth century. The music was on ⁴ '_____ ' made of aluminium foil. When people listened to the music a few times, the foil broke. Later, ⁵ _____ could hold longer ⁶ _____ and people could play them more often.

Gramophones were similar to phonographs, but they had the music on flat vinyl ⁷ _____ . The disks turned, and a ⁸ _____ or a small diamond 'took' the music off the record.

Sony ⁹ _____ the 'Walkman' in 1979. That made it possible to go for walks, travel or do sports and listen to music at the same time.

7 Study help

✱ Vocabulary: how to remember new words

a In your vocabulary notebook, record words in diagram form.

- Draw pictures next to the words. This will help you remember them.
- Add new words to your diagram when you meet them.
- Copy your diagram, with your book closed. How many words can you remember?

b Write the words in the correct places in the diagram.

> vinyl records
> a wax cylinder
> a gramophone

1 _____

2 _____

3 _____

Skills in mind

8 Read

Where is the true home of the hamburger?

The kind of beef we see in hamburgers, minced beef, was possibly invented by Mongolians over 800 years ago. But who first put the beef in between pieces of bread, and called it a hamburger?

Three different cities in the United States all say that they were the first to invent America's favourite food. Some people say that Fletcher Davis, from Athens, Texas, invented hamburgers. 'Old Dave', as people called him, was selling minced beef sandwiches in his lunch bar as early as the 1880s. Some years later, they say that a group of Germans called his sandwich a 'hamburger' because people from the German city of Hamburg ate this kind of beef.

Other people believe that the hamburger came from a different city called Hamburg – the 1885 fair in Hamburg, New York. The Menches brothers were selling pork sandwiches, but when there was no more pork, they used minced beef and gave it a new name, the 'hamburger'.

The third possible inventor of the hamburger was Charlie Nagreen, also known as 'Hamburger Charlie', from Seymour, Wisconsin. He said that in 1885 he invented the world's first hamburgers at a fair. Seymour now celebrates the invention of the hamburger every year. In 1989, it was the home of the world's largest ever burger – over 2,500 kg!

READING TIP

How to answer 'true', 'false' or 'not in the text' questions

- Look at the pictures and title of the text.
- Read the whole text. Then read the statements carefully.
- <u>Underline</u> the parts of the text with the information.

a Read the text and mark statements 1–3 *T* (true), *F* (false), or *N* (not in the text). Then read the notes below and check your answers.

1 Hamburgers use a kind of beef called 'minced beef'. ☐

2 Mongolians invented hamburgers over 800 years ago. ☐

3 The three stories about the invention of hamburgers are all true. ☐

- 'Minced beef' is another way of saying 'the kind of beef we see in hamburgers'. So 1 is *true*.

- The Mongolians invented minced beef over 800 years ago, not hamburgers. So 2 is *false*.

- The cities say their stories are true, but we don't know if the stories are really true, because the text does not give enough information. So for 3, *not in the text* is the correct answer.

b Read the rest of the text again. For statements 1–5, write *T* (true), *F* (false), or *N* (not in the text).

1 Fletcher Davis gave the name 'hamburger' to his minced beef sandwich. ☐ *F*

2 'Old Dave' visited Hamburg in Germany. ☐

3 There is a place called Hamburg in New York. ☐

4 The Menches brothers used beef in their sandwiches because no one liked pork. ☐

5 'Hamburger Charlie' and the Menches brothers say they invented hamburgers in the same year. ☐

9 Listen

 Listen and tick (✓) the correct picture.

1 What did the Menches brothers say they also invented?

a ☐   b ☐   c ✓

2 What did 'Old Dave' say he also invented?

a ☐   b ☐   c ☐

3 What did the man in England invent in 1750?

a ☐   b ☐   c ☐

4 What did Thomas Adams invent?

a ☐   b ☐   c ☐

Unit check

1 Fill in the spaces

Complete the text with the words in the box.

| get | was getting | got wet | got a horrible surprise | got to school |
| got up | didn't get | got nervous | didn't hear | was shining |

Yesterday wasn't my best day. First I ___got up___ late because I [1] _____ the alarm clock. Perhaps I should [2] _____ two alarm clocks! When I finally [3] _____ at half past nine, I [4] _____ – my class was doing a French test! I [5] _____ because I only had 20 minutes left to do the test. Unfortunately, I [6] _____ a single answer right! After school I felt better again, because the sun [7] _____ ! But when I [8] _____ close to home, it suddenly started to rain, so of course I [9] _____ !

`9`

2 Choose the correct answers

(Circle) the correct answer: a, b or c.

1 Our dog ran away while I _____ to Sarah.

   a talk   b talked   c (was talking)

2 We were in the garden when it _____ to rain.

   a was started   b started   c was starting

3 Jane _____ angry yesterday because we were late.

   a getting   b gets   c got

4 When I _____ about the prize, I got excited.

   a heard   b were hearing   c was hearing

5 The girls _____ when they saw the funny film.

   a laughed   b was laughing   c were laughing

6 I saw Alice a minute ago. She _____ on her mobile phone.

   a was talking   b talked   c were talking

7 When Pete and Simon _____ , we were all watching TV.

   a arrived   b arriving   c were arriving

8 The phone _____ , so I sent her an email.

   a wasn't working   b weren't working
   c didn't worked

9 When I got to the party, my friends _____ a great time.

   a was having   b had   c were having

`8`

3 Vocabulary

Complete the sentences with the words in the box.

| windscreen wipers | invented | engine | remote control | idea | a chance | dishwasher | surprise | got to |

1 Our new _dishwasher_ is not as noisy as the old one was.

2 Where is the _____ ? I want to change the channel on the TV.

3 It's starting to rain. Drive carefully and put on the _____ .

4 They have a diesel _____ to produce their own electricity.

5 Josephine Cochran hated doing the washing-up, so she _____ the dishwasher.

6 Our plane was delayed, so we _____ Istanbul very late.

7 While I was listening to my favourite piece of music, I suddenly got an _____ .

8 I'll phone you as soon as I get _____ .

9 My uncle lives in Australia, so when he arrived at our house, we got a real _____ !

`8`

How did you do?

Total: `25`

| | Very good 20 – 25 | | OK 14 – 19 |  | Review Unit 1 again 0 – 13 |

2 He ran faster

1 Remember and check

Complete the sentences with the words in the box. Then check with the information on page 18 of the Student's Book.

> shorter ~~fastest~~ best
> slower more than

1 In the 2008 Olympics Usain Bolt from Jamaica was the __fastest__ man in the 100 metre sprint.

2 Irish sprinter Jason Smyth was only a little _____ , but he won gold too.

3 In the women's discus, Marianne Buggenhagen's throw was _____ than Stefanie Brown Trafton's, but they both won gold.

4 Both Jason Smyth and Marianne Buggenhagen were the _____ athletes in the Paralympic Games.

5 At the Paralympics in Beijing there were _____ 4,000 athletes.

2 Grammar

✻ Comparative and superlative adjectives

a Circle the correct words.

1 She's *more younger / (younger)* than she looks.

2 This is *the worst / the most bad* day of my life!

3 Who is *the older / the oldest* man in the world?

4 My brother's *much tidier / tidiest* than me.

5 Is your house *more old / older* than mine?

6 I think Giacomo is *cleverer than / the cleverest* boy in the class.

b Complete the sentences. Use the comparative (+ *than*) or superlative form of the adjectives in the box.

> tall happy ~~beautiful~~ good
> expensive successful

1 My city is __the most beautiful__ city in the world!

2 The day I married your mother was wonderful. It was _____ day of my life!

3 Is Sears Tower _____ building in the world?

4 That was a great holiday! It was much _____ than last year.

5 It cost €2,500! It was _____ camera in the shop.

6 Bill Gates is one of _____ businessmen in the world.

✻ Intensifiers with comparatives

c Write a sentence about each picture in your notebook. Use the comparative and *much, far, a lot* or *a bit / a little*.

The meat is a bit more expensive than the chicken.

1 (A)  (B)

10 euros   9 euros

2 (A)   (B)

Today: 16°C   Yesterday: 21°C

3 (A)    (B)

Ferrari, 230 km/h   Fiat, 150 km/h

4 (A)   (B)

Mrs James, 32   Mr James, 51

3 Vocabulary
✱ Antonyms

a Complete the puzzle. Write the antonyms of the adjectives that the pictures show.

1	o	l	d					
2								
3								
4			f	a	t			
5					g			
6								
7								
8	b	r	i	l	l	i	a	n	t
9									

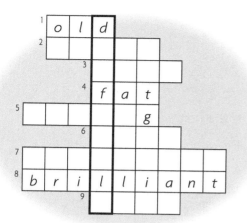

b What is the antonym of the mystery word in the middle? _____

4 Grammar
✱ (not) as ... as

a Match the sentences with the same meaning.

1 Carol isn't as tall as Ruth.
2 Carol is as tall as Ruth.
3 Carol isn't as short as Ruth.
4 Carol isn't as old as Ruth.
5 Carol is as old as Ruth.
6 Carol isn't as young as Ruth.

a Ruth is 1.20 m and Carol is 1.25 m.
b Ruth is 15 years old and Carol is 14 years old.
c Ruth is 10 years old and Carol is 11 years old.
d Ruth is 1.65 m and Carol is 1.58 m.
e Ruth is 1.65 m and Carol is 1.65 m.
f Ruth is 15 years old and Carol is 15 years old.

b Write sentences using (not) as ... as to describe the pictures.

Jane *is as happy as her sister.*
(happy)

John _____
_____ . (tall)

The TV _____
_____ . (expensive)

The cat _____
_____ . (thin)

Arsenal _____
_____ . (good)

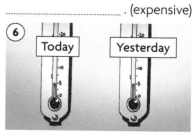

Today _____
_____ . (cold)

5 Grammar

✷ Adverbs/comparative adverbs

a Write the adverbs for these adjectives.

1 quick ...._quickly_.........   5 fast ....

2 slow ....   6 bad ....

3 easy ....   7 good ....

4 happy ....   8 hard ....

b Complete the second sentence so it means the same as the first.

1 His German isn't very good.

    He doesn't speak _German well._

2 He had to be fast to catch the bus. He had to run

    ....

3 He's a very slow driver. He ....
....

4 His writing isn't clear. He doesn't ....
....

5 My secretary's typing is quick. My secretary
....

6 The test was very easy for me. I did ....
....

c Paul, David, Fred and Richard all go to the same school. Read the sentences about them and complete the table with the information.

1 Paul is taller than Fred but not as tall as Richard.
2 David runs faster than Fred.
3 David is the shortest.
4 The tallest boy is also the richest.
5 Richard speaks French better than Paul.
6 David is richer than Fred.
7 Fred speaks French the best.
8 Paul isn't as rich as Fred.
9 The richest boy runs more slowly than David and Fred, but not as slowly as Paul.
10 The boy who has got £200 speaks French better than the tallest boy.

	Paul	David	Fred	Richard
Height: 1.5 m, 1.6 m, 1.7 m, 1.8 m				1.8 m
Money in the bank: £50, £100, £200, £500				
Grade in French test: A, B, C, F				
Position in school Olympics 100m: 1st, 2nd, 3rd, 4th				

6 Pronunciation

✷ _than_ and _as_

a ▶ CD3 T10 Listen and write down the phrases you hear.

1 ...._as good as gold_.........   3 ....   5 ....

2 ....   4 ....   6 ....

b ▶ CD3 T10 How do you say the phrases in Exercise 6a in your language? Listen again and repeat.

7 Vocabulary

✴ Sport

a Complete the sentences with the words in the box.

draw   nil   ~~won~~   beat   champions

1 Last night Spain _won_ two–_____ against Brazil. The Spanish team were brillant! I think they will be the _____ .

2 My dad is really good at chess. He _____ me again yesterday!

3 In the end, we didn't win or lose. It was a _____ .

b **Vocabulary bank** Match the words with their definitions.

1 to draw
2 to substitute
3 a record
4 a championship
5 to score

a to use a player for part of a game instead of another player
b in sports: to do something better than it was done before
c to finish with the same number of points/goals as the other player/team
d to win or obtain a point, goal, etc.
e a sports competition to decide who is the best

8 Everyday English

Complete the dialogues. Use the expressions in the box.

guess what   that sort of thing   at the end of the day   ~~an awful lot of~~   we're talking about   that's not the point

1 A: You want £200 for your bike? That's ¹ _an awful lot of_ money, Jake.

   B: I know it is. But ² _____ a really good bike here, Andy.

2 A: That new girl Sarah's really good-looking. And ³ _____ ? Her father's really rich, too!

   B: But ⁴ _____ , Paul. The important thing is that she's a nice person.

3 A: I'm going to be really lazy next weekend – relax, read books, watch TV, ⁵ _____ .

   B: Good idea. ⁶ _____ , you can't work all the time, can you?

9 Study help

✴ How to get good study habits

a There are many ways you can practise and improve your English outside the classroom. Look at the pictures and mark how often you do the activities (O = often; S = sometimes; N = never).

b Match pictures A–F with the advice.

1 80% of the internet is in English. You could try reading interesting texts in English, or try websites that help you improve your English. ☐

2 Get an English-speaking penfriend! ☐

3 Buy an English language magazine or newspaper regularly. ☐

4 Buy or borrow a reader that is the right level for you. Good stories that are not too difficult are a great help. ☐

5 Videos and DVDs are a fun way to practise your listening. With a DVD you can watch a scene in your own language first, and then watch it in English. ☐

6 Listen to a song in English and write down everything you understand. Then go online and check the lyrics on the internet. ☐

10 Listen

▶ **CD3 T11** Phil went to the World Cup Final in 2006. James talks to him about it. Listen and ⟨circle⟩ the correct answers.

1 What did Phil enjoy most about the game?
  a the football   b ⟨the penalties at the end⟩   c the stadium

2 How long after the end of the match did they leave the stadium?
  a an hour   b 30 minutes   c two hours

3 Where did they go afterwards?
  a to their hotel   b to an Italian restaurant   c to a fast food restaurant

11 Write

Rewrite the text to make it more interesting. Use the ideas in the Writing tip.

> It was 10 pm and I was late for the party. I got in my car. I drove to the party. A dog ran into the road. I saw the dog. I tried to stop. I lost control of the car. I hit a tree.

WRITING TIP

Making your writing more interesting

a **Read these two descriptions. Which is more interesting and why?**

> 1 Three years ago I went to Germany to see the World Cup Final. It was a very good experience. We were very excited. We arrived at the stadium five hours early. There were lots of people outside the stadium. A lot of the people were dancing and singing. We went into the stadium and went to our seats.
>
> 2 Three years ago I went to Germany to see the World Cup Final. It was a fantastic experience! We were really excited so we arrived at the huge, modern stadium five hours early. There were thousands of happy people outside and a lot of them were dancing and singing excitedly. We went inside and couldn't wait to get to our seats.

1 Think about the language you want to use. Is there a more interesting or dramatic way of saying what you want to say? How does the writer in text 2 say: *It was a very good experience*; *lots of people*; *we went to our seats*?

2 Add details to your writing. One way to do this is to use adjectives and adverbs. In text 2, how does the writer describe: *the stadium*; *the people*; *the dancing and singing*? Underline the adjectives and adverbs in text 2.

3 Too many short sentences can sound boring. Link some of them together with words like *and*, *so*, *because*, *while*, *but*, etc. ⟨Circle⟩ the linking words in text 2.

4 Try not to repeat the same words too often. How does the writer in text 2 say: *a lot of the people*; *We went into the stadium*?

b **Rewrite the sentences to make them more interesting. Use the ideas in the tips.**

1 She walked into the room and sat down in the chair. (tip 2)

    She walked into the dark room slowly and sat down in the comfortable chair.

2 My alarm clock didn't ring. I was late for work. (tip 3)

    _____.

3 The meal was great. (tip 1)

    _____.

4 My favourite restaurant is an Italian restaurant. The restaurant is the best restaurant in town. (tip 4)

    _____.

Unit check

1 Fill in the spaces

Complete the text with the antonyms of the words in brackets.

Mum had a go at me this morning. 'Your room is so __messy__ (tidy). It must be [1] _____ (easy) for you to find your way to the door!', she said. I didn't say a word – I was [2] _____ (noisy). My room is always [3] _____ (messy). Well, there are some things on the floor. But the door's [4] _____ (far) my bed, so it's really [5] _____ (difficult) for me to find my way to the door. I think a tidy room is really [6] _____ (interesting). When I look for my things, I always find something else. Yesterday I was looking for my [7] _____ (old) football boots. I couldn't find them, but I found a photo of my sister. She looked really [8] _____ (old)!

[8]

2 Choose the correct answers

Circle the correct answer: a, b or c.

1   Tennis is more interesting _____ football.
    a than   b as   c when

2   I read that women are _____ drivers than men.
    a as good   b the best   c better

3   He plays the guitar really _____ .
    a well   b bad   c good

4   My Italian is quite _____ , but I can't speak it fluently.
    a good   b well   c better

5   Tom is _____ I am. We are both 15.
    a old   b older than   c as old as

6   Read this book. It will help you to play football much _____ .
    a good   b better   c well

7   This test is no problem. I can do it _____ .
    a easily   b easy   c easiest

8   People say Chinese is the _____ language to learn.
    a difficult   b more difficult   c most difficult

9   I live _____ away from school than all my friends.
    a further   b the furthest   c far

[8]

3 Vocabulary

Complete the sentences with a word or phrase from the box.

| as fast   most interesting   ~~more useful~~   drew   nil   best   referee   messy   easy   noisy |

1   For me, a new mobile phone is __more useful__ than a new watch.
2   Meet Cindy – she is my _____ friend.
3   The test was so _____ that it only took me ten minutes to finish!
4   In big cities, riding a bike can be _____ as driving a car.
5   My team lost, five-_____ . I can't believe it!
6   The _____ sent one of the players off for foul play.
7   Both teams played very well, and in the end they _____ .
8   Suddenly it was so _____ in the cave that we were all scared.
9   For me, Geography is the _____ subject. I love it!
10 I should tidy up my room – it's so _____ .

[9]

How did you do?

Total: [25]

| 😊 | Very good 20 – 25 | 😐 | OK 14 – 19 | 😞 | Review Unit 2 again 0 – 13 |

3 Our world

1 Remember and check

Match the two parts of the sentences. Then check with the text on page 26 of the Student's Book.

1 For a long time, Paris had a big problem
2 Now the Velib scheme might help
3 It allows people to take a bike and
4 You can get the bikes
5 The Velib scheme might also
6 Temperatures will continue to rise

a to reduce pollution levels in the atmosphere.
b from one of the 1,450 bike stations.
c help people to live more healthily.
d with pollution from exhaust fumes.
e unless we do something now about pollution.
f ride it for as long as they want.

2 Grammar

✱ will/won't, and might / may (not) for prediction

a Match the sentences with the pictures. Write 1–6 in the boxes.

1 Hurry up, Tom. You'll be late!
2 Don't go up there – you might fall.
3 I don't feel well. I may not come to the party tonight.
4 I won't be long – I'm almost ready.
5 Listen, we're lost – I think we might be a bit late.
6 Now just relax – this won't hurt.

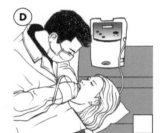

b Read the sentences. Then write C (certain) or P (possible) in the boxes.

1 People won't read real books in the future – only things from the Internet. ☐ C
2 Let's get this video – it may be good. ☐
3 You'll speak English really well after a year in Britain. ☐
4 I might see you at the party later. ☐
5 John won't be at school tomorrow – he's ill. ☐
6 Temperatures might not rise in the future. ☐
7 There may not be enough food at home. ☐

c Match the two parts of the sentences.

1 Is that the phone? It may be John,
2 I might not have enough money
3 You won't have time to call Matt,
4 I might not go to university,
5 There might be life on other planets,
6 Jeans will never
7 I may study Spanish next year

a because I forgot to go to the bank.
b we're already late!
c but no one really knows.
d because I don't want to study any more.
e go out of fashion.
f and my friend knows a good teacher.
g he promised to call me tonight.

d Complete the sentences. Use *'ll/won't* or *might / might not* and the verb in brackets.

1 Maria _won't be_ (not be) at the party yet. It's too early. (certain)
2 I _____ (go) to the cinema tonight. I'm not sure. (possible)
3 I _____ (not do) my homework tonight. I'm feeling very tired! (possible)
4 There _____ (be) some great music at the party. I'm the DJ! (certain)
5 It _____ (not take) as long as you think. Let's start now. (possible)
6 We _____ (have) time for some chips before the game. (possible)
7 He _____ (not do) very well in his exams. He never does any work. (certain)
8 It _____ (be) a great concert. That band is fantastic! (certain)

3 Vocabulary

✱ The environment

a Read the definitions. Then write the words next to the anagrams.

1	Wet, tropical places with lots of trees	arinfrostes	_rainforests_
2	Dirty gas from cars and factories	fesum	_____
3	We find this in air or water	lotilupon	_____
4	The gases around our planet	rapseemhot	_____
5	A big building that produces energy	wrope oatsnit	_____
6	Using old glass, plastic and paper again	cringlecy	_____
7	Things you don't want any more	shrubib	_____
8	Bits of paper, empty cans, etc. on the street	retilt	_____

b Match the two parts of the sentences.

1 If we want our planet to survive, we need to stop   a recycle them!
2 Electricity is very expensive, so don't   b pick it up!
3 Is that your empty crisp packet on the ground? Please   c polluting it.
4 Don't throw away your old bottles and newspapers! Please   d drop it everywhere!
5 Have you heard about the trees in our street? They're going to   e cleaned it up.
6 People in my school don't care about litter. They just   f waste it.
7 Our river was very dirty before they   g cut them down!

c Complete the text with the words in the box.

> recycle   cutting   forests   rubbish   clean   fumes   pollution   warming   picking   litter

It's Your Planet

Why don't you care about your world? It is difficult to see what you can do to stop people _cutting_ down hundreds of trees every day in the [1] _____ , or how you can stop all the [2] _____ from traffic and factories that cause [3] _____ in the atmosphere and global [4] _____ .

But you can do little things yourself. Can you say that you never drop [5] _____ on the streets? You could always try [6] _____ up the things that other people drop, especially in our parks. They might learn from your actions.

Just think of all the money we'll save if we don't need to pay people to [7] _____ up the streets. And there's no need to put your empty cola cans in the [8] _____ for someone to collect every week. Why not [9] _____ your cans, bottles, plastic and paper? Then we'll all have a cleaner planet.

4 Grammar

★ First conditional

a Complete the text. Use *will* or *won't* (if appropriate) and the correct form of the verbs in brackets.

How coral reefs die

Did you know that coral in the sea will die if people
cut down (cut down) more rainforests? It happens like this.
If people [1]_____ (cut down) more rainforests, the
world's temperature [2]_____ (rise).

If the temperature of the sea [3]_____ (go up) too, the
small animals and plants that coral lives on [4]_____
(start) to die. So, the coral [5]_____ (not get) enough
food, and then it will go white and die. If the coral
[6]_____ (die), over 90,000 different kinds of fish
[7]_____ (be) in danger of dying too. So, as you can see,
one natural disaster often causes another one.

b Put the words in order to make sentences or questions.

1 won't / pass / exams / your / hard / don't / if / you / you / work
   You won't pass your exams if you don't work hard.

2 buy / a / if / you / present / I'm / will / me / good
   _____ ?

3 message / see / your / if / give / James / I'll / I / him
   _____ .

4 late / they / if / rains / arrive / will / it
   _____ ?

5 do / what / you / will / if / doesn't / he / phone
   _____ ?

6 sister / lend / if / her / ask / I / will / mobile / me / my / her
   _____ .

7 money / give / some / haven't / if / any / got / I'll / you / you
   _____ .

★ if/unless

c (Circle) the correct words.

1 I'll give you some of my chocolate (if) / unless you give me some ice cream.

2 Unless / If you read the instructions, you won't know how to play the game.

3 Will you give Marco my message unless / if you see him?

4 If / Unless the phone rings while I'm in the shower, will you answer it?

5 Your dad won't be very happy if / unless he finds out what you did.

6 We'll be late unless / if we leave right now.

d Complete the sentences with your own ideas.

1 I'll go out this weekend if
   _____
   _____ .

2 If I'm hungry on the way home from school, _____
   _____ .

3 I'll be happy tomorrow if
   _____
   _____ .

4 If the weather is bad this weekend, _____
   _____ .

5 I won't talk to my best friend if
   _____
   _____ .

6 If I can't watch TV tonight,
   _____
   _____ .

7 I'll make my own dinner tonight if _____
   _____ .

8 If I can't do my English homework, _____
   _____ .

5 Pronunciation

✷ *won't* and *might*

▶ CD3 T12 Listen and <u>underline</u> the sentences you hear. Then listen again and repeat.

1 They want to come. / <u>They won't come</u>.

2 They want to go to bed. / They won't go to bed.

3 I won't be here. / I want to be here.

4 So you won't play squash? / So you want to play squash?

5 I think you're maybe right. / I think you might be right.

6 You said you might teach her. / You said you're my teacher.

6 Culture in mind

Complete the summary about water with the phrases in the box.

| ~~for our survival~~   we cannot get to   needs to be moist   polar ice caps |
| called evaporation   have access to   use one per cent |

Water is very important *for our survival* on the planet. Most water is salt water. Of all the fresh water, we can only ¹_____ . The other 99 per cent is in places ²_____ . 70 per cent of that water is frozen in the ³_____ . Most of the remaining 30 per cent is in the ground. The soil ⁴_____ so trees and plants can grow. There are also huge underground lakes that we don't ⁵_____ . When it rains, about two-thirds of the water goes back up into the atmosphere through a process ⁶_____ .

7 Study help

✷ Word formation

When you learn a new word, it is a good idea to learn the different parts of speech. English has many different ways to make verbs, nouns and adjectives.

a Look at these examples with the word *help*:

Noun: Can you give me **some help** with my homework?

Verb: Sometimes I **help** my parents cook dinner.

Adjective: Using a dictionary **is helpful** if you want to know the different forms of a word.

b A good dictionary will give you information about the different forms of a word, and example sentences. Look at the example from the *Cambridge Learner's Dictionary*. What part of speech is *environment*? *noun*
What is the adjective? *environmental*

○━**environment** /ɪn'vaɪərᵊnmənt/ *noun* **1 the environment** the air, land, and water where people, animals, and plants live *The new road may cause damage to the environment.* ➲ *See usage note at* **nature**. **2** [C] the situation that you live or work in, and how it influences how you feel *We are working in a very competitive environment.*
environmental /ɪnˌvaɪərᵊn'mentᵊl/ *adj* relating to the environment *environmental damage* ● *an environmental disaster* ● **environmentally** *adv environmentally damaging chemicals*

c Complete the table.

Noun	Verb	Adjective
1 _____	2 _____	polluted
energy	✗	3 _____
power	✗	4 _____
waste	5 _____	6 _____
7 _____	increase	✗
8 _____	warm (up)	9 _____
10 _____	11 _____	recyclable

d Use your dictionary to check your answers.

Skills in mind

8 Listen

▶ **CD3 T13** Mike is talking about school. Listen and tick (✓) the things Mike likes and cross (✗) the things he doesn't like.

1 sports facilities ✓   4 the length of the lessons ☐
2 school meals ☐   5 the school uniform ☐
3 the teachers ☐   6 school rules ☐

9 Read and write

a Read the text and answer the questions.

Make Aston Fields High School a better place!

Do you ever complain about school to your family and friends? Maybe about the lessons, or the school facilities, or meals? We all have bad things to say sometimes (even teachers!). But we can't just complain. A better idea is to say what you think is wrong and why, and to make suggestions so that things can improve.

So enter our competition. Write an article for the school website and tell us what you think is wrong with our school, explain the problems and say what you think we can do about it.

This is not homework! The best article will win **100 euros**. So get writing now!

1 What things about a school do people sometimes complain about? Give three examples.

_____
_____ .

2 What do students who enter the competition have to do?

_____ .

3 What will the winner of the competition receive?

_____ .

b Read Jen's reply. Do you think Jen should win? Why / Why not?

_____ .

Right. Some lessons are really boring. All my friends say the same. My dad says why don't we have more lessons with computers and stuff? I don't know if he's right, really.

And another thing. PE lessons are boring – it's all netball, netball, netball! I hate netball. Why can't we do things I like – gym, or dancing or something?

Oh, and I nearly forgot. At lunchtime they tell everyone to go outside. That's crazy! What's wrong with people staying in the main hall? You don't use it for anything. Then we could play chess and stuff, or I could do my homework (or not!).

So, what about it?

Jen

WRITING TIP

Using linkers

Jen didn't win the prize! Her ideas are good, but her style is not appropriate. Writing an article is not the same as writing an email.

a Jen rewrote her article. Put the paragraphs in order. Look at her first article.

☐ Secondly, not everyone in our school likes netball.

☐ Finally, why can't we use the main hall at lunchtime?

1 First of all, many people think that interactive lessons with computers could make school more interesting.

6 To sum up, I believe that these things will make our school a better place.

☐ We could have other activities in PE lessons – gym or dancing, for instance.

☐ Some people want to play quiet games like chess, or just do their homework, but they don't have a place to go.

b What words does Jen use to:

● start her first idea?

_____

● start her second idea?

_____

● start her last main idea?

_____

● give examples of activities?

_____

● introduce her closing sentence?

_____

c Write your entry to the competition.

Unit check

1 Fill in the spaces

Complete the text with the words in the box.

~~pollution~~ waste environment litter pollute may not fumes atmosphere recycle will

I live in a big city. There are lots of cars and a lot of air ___pollution___ . Near my city, there is a big factory, and the ¹ _____ are a real problem. They ² _____ the air and the water.

Today, we have big problems with the ³ _____ , but I think life in the future ⁴ _____ be really different. There ⁵ _____ be any nuclear power stations, and most countries might only use renewable energy. This will be positive for the planet's ⁶ _____ . People won't drop ⁷ _____ in the streets, or ⁸ _____ water. We will all ⁹ _____ bottles and other rubbish.

| 9 |

2 Choose the correct answers

Circle the correct answer: a, b or c.

1 I think I _____ an umbrella with me.

  a take b 'll take c not take

2 I promise I _____ study all day tomorrow.

  a might b 'll c not

3 I don't think Karen _____ come to the meeting.

  a might not b doesn't c will

4 If she hears what you said, she _____ angry.

  a might b are c 'll be

5 If we _____ more rainforests, our planet will be in danger.

  a are cutting down b 'll cut down c cut down

6 Unless she helps me, I _____ her to the party.

  a might invite b won't invite

  c don't invite

7 There'll be problems if we _____ more renewable energy.

  a won't use b don't use c 'll use

8 What will Tom do if his friends _____ to him any more?

  a don't talk b talk c will talk

9 If the weather is nice, I _____ and see you.

  a coming b may come c come

| 8 |

3 Vocabulary

Circle the correct options.

1 In some *developing countries* / *polar ice caps* there is very little clean water.

2 The pet food factory *cuts down* / *pollutes* a lot of our town's water.

3 People are *cutting down* / *polluting* more and more of the trees in the rainforests.

4 It took them a long time to *clean up* / *cut down* the oil from that beach.

5 They're building a new *traffic jam* / *power station* near our town.

6 We should do everything we can so we don't *drop* / *waste* water.

7 Lots of illnesses are the result of poor *recycling* / *sanitation*.

8 Recycling *rubbish* / *fumes* can save a lot of resources.

9 Don't drop litter – keep your *environment* / *waste* clean!

| 8 |

How did you do?

Total: | 25 |

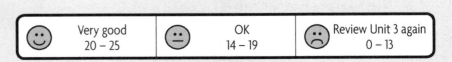

| 😊 | Very good 20 – 25 | 😐 | OK 14 – 19 | 🙁 | Review Unit 3 again 0 – 13 |

4 Holiday or vacation?

1 Remember and check

(Circle) the correct answers. Then check with the text on page 32 of the Student's Book.

1 Canada is ... the USA, but only 30 million people live there.
   a as big as   b (much bigger than)   c not much bigger than

2 The biggest city in Canada is ...
   a Toronto.   b Vancouver.   c Montreal.

3 ... is a city in British Columbia.
   a Alberta   b Toronto   c Vancouver

4 The most popular sport in Canada is ...
   a baseball.   b ice hockey.   c basketball.

5 English and Chinese are the most common languages in ...
   a Montreal.   b Ontario.   c Vancouver.

6 It's about 1,200 kilometres from Vancouver to ...
   a New York.   b Los Angeles.   c San Francisco.

2 Grammar
✱ Question tags

a Complete the sentences with the question tags in the box.

> didn't they   can she   haven't they   doesn't he
> ~~does he~~   can't she   aren't we

1 He doesn't know the answer, _does he_ ?
2 We're really late, _____ ?
3 She can wait, _____ ?
4 They knew all the answers, _____ ?
5 Your father works in that office, _____ ?
6 Your sister can't cook, _____ ?
7 They've finished their test, _____ ?

b If the question tag is correct, write (✓). If it is incorrect, write (✗) and correct it.

1 It's a nice day, isn't it? ✓ _____
2 He lives round here, isn't it? ✗ _doesn't he_
3 They're Spanish, aren't they? ☐ _____
4 Your brother studies Maths, don't he? ☐ _____
5 You went to Paris last year, went you? ☐ _____
6 They won't be late, will they? ☐ _____
7 She's got a boyfriend, isn't she? ☐ _____
8 They shouldn't do that, shouldn't they? ☐ _____

c Complete the dialogue with the correct question tags.

Steve: Jane, you play the guitar, _don't you_ ?

Jane: A little, but I'm not good!

S: But you played at the school concert, [1] _____ ?

J: Yes. Why?

S: You'll play at my party, [2] _____ ?

J: Well, OK. But Mike's going to be there, [3] _____ ? And he can play really well, [4] _____ ?

S: I think so. But that isn't important, [5] _____ ?

J: Yes, it is! He's much better than me, so you should ask him to play, [6] _____ ?

3 Pronunciation
✱ Question tags: intonation

a ▶ CD3 T14 Listen and write the question tags.

1 You're American, _aren't you_ ?   D

2 You're American, _aren't you_ ?   U

3 She goes to your school, _____ ?   ☐

4 They don't live round here, _____ ?   ☐

5 I can come, _____ ?   ☐

6 You'll help me, _____ ?   ☐

b ▶ CD3 T14 Listen again. Does the voice go up or down at the end of each tag? Write *U* or *D*. Then listen and repeat.

4 Vocabulary

✱ British vs. North American English

a Complete the table.

British English		North American English
1 *pavement*		*sidewalk*
2 _____		_____
3 _____		_____
4 _____		_____
5 _____	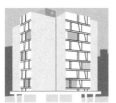	_____
6 _____		_____

b Look at the pictures and complete the sentences.

1 John, can you put the _rubbish_ out, please?

2 Come on, Ann. Let's go up in the _____ .

3 I really like travelling on the _____ .

4 Yeah! I'm going on _____ to Hawaii!

5 I need to buy some new _____ .

6 Hey! Don't ride your bike on the _____ !

c **Vocabulary bank** Underline the American English words. Write the words in British English.

1 I was surprised to see that my aunt didn't have any baggage. _luggage_

2 They're going to start building their new house in the fall. _____

3 Can you draw the drapes, please? The sun's really bright. _____

4 There was a monkey sitting on the hood of our car. _____

5 Can you open the trunk of the car, please? I want to put the bags in. _____

6 When we got to the bus stop we saw a long line of people. _____

5 Grammar

✳ Present perfect simple, *already* and *yet*

a Complete the table with the past simple and past participle forms of the irregular verbs.

Base form	Past simple	Past participle
be	was/were	1 _____
begin	2 _____	3 _____
come	came	4 _____
drink	5 _____	drunk
eat	6 _____	eaten
go	went	7 _____
know	8 _____	9 _____
see	saw	10 _____
write	11 _____	12 _____

b Match the sentences with the pictures. Write numbers 1–6 in the boxes.

1 I've already eaten my dinner.
2 I haven't eaten my dinner yet.
3 They've already gone to bed.
4 They haven't gone to bed yet.
5 She's already seen the film.
6 She hasn't seen the film yet.

c Complete the sentences with *yet* or *already*.

1 I haven't finished my homework _____*yet*_____ .

2 Have you heard their new CD _____ ?

3 We've _____ read that magazine.

4 She hasn't left school _____ .

5 My parents haven't come back _____ .

6 I know that joke – you've _____ told it to me!

7 They haven't had dinner _____ .

8 Have you brushed your teeth _____ ?

d Write the sentences and questions. Use the present perfect and *already* or *yet*.

1 A: Alan, you / finish your dinner?

   Alan, have you finished your dinner yet?

   B: I / eat the hamburger, but I / not finish the vegetables.

   I have already eaten the hamburger, but I haven't finished the vegetables yet.

2 A: Maria / go to Sally's house?

   _____
   _____ .

   B: Yes, but she / not come back.

   _____
   _____ .

3 A: I / buy the new Killers CD.

   _____
   _____ .

   B: Really? you / listen to it?

   _____
   _____ .

4 A: you / go to sleep?

   _____
   _____ .

   B: No! And you / ask me three times!

   _____
   _____ .

6 Grammar

✱ Present perfect simple with *just*

a Write *just* in the correct place in each sentence.

1 He's come home. *He's just come home.*

2 I've phoned Jenny. _____ .

3 We've arrived. _____ .

4 My parents have gone out. _____ .

5 The film's finished. _____ .

b Look at the pictures. Write sentences using the present perfect with *just* and *yet*.

1 buy a magazine / read it

He's just bought a magazine,
but he hasn't read it yet.

2 buy an ice cream / eat it

_____
_____ .

3 write a letter / post it

_____
_____ .

4 buy a new CD / listen to it

_____
_____ .

8 Study help

✱ How to remember verbs

Make word cards that you can carry with you. Here is an example using past forms of irregular verbs.

● Get some small pieces of card. On one side of each card, write an irregular English verb. On the other side, write the past simple and past participle forms.

| throw | | threw, thrown |

● Carry the cards in your pocket or bag. When you have time, take a card, look at the verb and try to remember the two past forms. Turn the card over and check. If you were right, throw the card away. If you were wrong, put the card back and try again later.

7 Everyday English

Complete the dialogue. Use the expressions in the box.

> ~~What do you reckon~~
> no wonder
> the kind of thing
> Have a look
> you're not supposed to
> in the middle of

Paul: I'm a bit bored. Let's watch something on TV. *What do you reckon* ?

Sarah: OK. Is there anything good on?

Paul: I'm not sure.
¹ _____ in the TV magazine.

Sarah: OK. Hmm. No, there's nothing very interesting. There's never anything good on ² _____ the afternoon.

Paul: Oh look! There's a science fiction film from the 1960s! Let's watch that.

Sarah: No – that's not
³ _____ I like watching.

Paul: Come on, Sarah. They're funny! I watch them all the time.

Sarah: Really? Well,
⁴ _____
you've got square eyes, from watching so much TV.

Paul: I haven't got square eyes! Sarah, ⁵ _____ say things like that to me!

Sarah: I'm only joking, Paul. OK – let's watch the film. What's it called? *Plan 9 from Outer Space*? Oh no!

Skills in mind

LISTENING TIP

Listening and choosing pictures

Sometimes you have to listen to a recording and look at pictures. While you listen, you have to either:

- tick the pictures that show things that the people talk about

or:

- choose from sets of pictures that are similar to each other.

1 Look at the pictures carefully before you listen. What do the pictures show? What are the things called in English? If there are pairs of pictures, how are they different from each other?

2 Listen the first time. Do you hear any of the words in English that you thought of in question 1?

3 If you are sure about a picture, tick (✓) it. If you aren't sure, listen again.

4 Remember: you don't have to understand **everything** to choose the correct picture(s). Listen for the **key words**.

9 Listen

a ▶ **CD3 T15** Josh has been on a trip to the USA. Listen to him talking to Sally about his trip. Tick (✓) the things in the pictures he talks about.

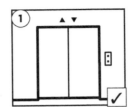

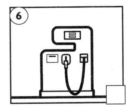

b ▶ **CD3 T16** Match the words. Then listen again and check.

British English	North American English
1 lift	a truck
2 bill	b gas
3 tap	c check
4 petrol	d elevator
5 lorry	e faucet

10 Write

a You are going on holiday to the UK. You are going to stay with an English family in London and study English at a school there. Look at the list of things you need to do before you go.

A tick (✓) means you have already done it. A cross (✗) means you haven't done it yet.

b Write an email to your penfriend in England. Tell him/her about your trip and about your preparations for it. Use the list and add more ideas if you want to.

Buy a plane ticket (✓)

Get a passport (✗)

Write to the family you are going to stay with (✓)

Write to the language school and book a place there (✓)

Get a letter from the school saying that you are going to be a student there (✗)

Buy some new clothes (✗)

Find out how to get from the airport to the English family (✗)

Buy a guide book of London (✓)

Unit check

1 Fill in the spaces

Complete this email from an American teen to a friend in the UK. Use the words in the box.

> apartment   have you heard   the kind of thing   have a look
> popular   subway   garbage   already   yet   ~~just~~

Dear Karen

Guess what! I've _just_ bought a new CD – it's by Avril Lavigne. She's really ¹ _____ here. ² _____ any of her music? I haven't listened to all the songs on the CD ³ _____ but I think it's great – I love it!

My big news is that we're going to move soon. My mum and dad don't like our ⁴ _____ any more. They've ⁵ _____ bought a house, and it's great! I'll have my own bedroom, and I can take the ⁶ _____ to go to school. There's a photo of the house on my blog – ⁷ _____ at it! Well, I must go now. I have to go and take the ⁸ _____ out. Ugh! It's ⁹ _____ I really hate doing! Well, write to me soon and tell me how you are, OK?

Janice

| 9 |

2 Choose the correct answers

(Circle) the correct answer: a, b or c.

1 Lisa _____ to Tom yet.

  a spoken   b spoke   c (hasn't spoken)

2 I _____ what I'll do in my holidays.

  a decide   b haven't decided   c decided

3 I haven't washed the car _____ .

  a just   b already   c yet

4 You've read that book, _____ you?

  a have   b hadn't   c haven't

5 The capital of Germany is Berlin, _____ ?

  a isn't it   b doesn't it   c hasn't it

6 I've just seen Kate, but I _____ to her yet.

  a haven't spoken   b didn't speak   c don't speak

7 Tony and Sarah have just moved to London, _____ ?

  a haven't they   b didn't they   c aren't they

8 You haven't got a new car, _____ ?

  a have you   b isn't it   c haven't you

9 He doesn't live in Vancouver, _____ ?

  a doesn't he   b isn't he   c does he | 8 |

3 Vocabulary

Find the words in American English for the words in the box. (→ or ↓)

> ~~biscuits~~   rubbish   lorry
> pavement   flat   trousers
> sweets   lift   underground

V	O	T	R	U	C	K	A	C	V	E
M	C	J	G	R	W	Q	H	O	G	L
K	A	X	A	O	W	K	T	O	R	E
Y	N	W	R	U	S	K	Q	K	O	V
M	D	Q	B	B	G	L	B	I	T	A
Z	Y	H	A	D	K	A	Y	E	A	T
N	E	J	G	P	A	N	T	S	V	O
J	T	S	E	A	U	E	N	V	E	R
T	S	I	D	E	W	A	L	K	F	D
G	F	R	F	N	R	D	D	B	L	A
S	S	U	B	W	A	Y	S	Y	E	P
A	P	A	R	T	M	E	N	T	R	A

| 8 |

How did you do?

Total: | 25 |

| 😊 Very good 20 – 25 | 😐 OK 14 – 19 | 😞 Review Unit 4 again 0 – 13 |

5 Growing up

1 Remember and check

Match the two parts of the sentences. Then check with the text on page 40 of the Student's Book.

1 The Niowra of Papua New Guinea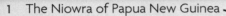
2 When boys become men, they are
3 It is a frightening place, full of
4 Then the boys are treated very badly
5 The boys play the drums together
6 When the ceremony is over, the boys

a taken to a hut called 'The Crocodile Nest'.
b several times a day for six weeks.
c to feel that they are not alone.
d crocodile teeth and skulls.
e are given adult responsibilities in the village.
f believe that crocodiles created the world.

2 Grammar

✱ Present simple passive

a Complete the sentences with the words in the box.

> is grown   are grown   's made
> are made   's written
> are written   is visited   are visited

1 My watch is cheap; it_'s made_ of plastic.
2 A lot of coffee .... in Brazil.
3 The Hard Rock Café .... by thousands of tourists every day.
4 I can't read this book because it .... in Spanish.
5 Those computers .... in Taiwan.
6 Some cities in Europe .... by millions of people every year.
7 Millions of emails .... every day.
8 Oranges .... in many hot countries.

b Here are some signs in English. Match the beginnings and endings of the signs.

1 English …
2 Foreign money …
3 Colour films …
4 Fresh food …
5 Cameras …
6 English lessons …

a repaired here.
b developed here.
c given here.
d spoken here.
e changed here.
f served here.

c Signs like these are often written without the verb *to be*. Write the complete sentences. Put the verb *to be* in the correct form.

1 _English is spoken here._
2 ....
3 ....
4 ....
5 ....
6 ....

d Rewrite the sentences using the present simple passive.

1 They collect 20,000 tonnes of rubbish every year.

20,000 tonnes of rubbish _are collected every year._

2 They sell a new computer every day.

A new computer _____ .

3 They design computer programs in that company.

Computer programs _____ .

4 People make mistakes in grammar exercises.

Mistakes _____ .

5 They build a lot of new houses every year.

_____ .

6 They often play football on Saturdays.

_____ .

3 Vocabulary

✲ Describing a person's age

a Find and (circle) the words to describe people's ages. Then write them in the correct order in the spaces. Use the pictures to help you.

teenagerchildpensionerbabytoddleradult

1 _____teenager_____   4 _____

2 _____   5 _____

3 _____   6 _____

b Complete the sentences. Use words from Exercise 3a.

1 In many countries, you become an __adult__ when you're 18 years old.

2 My older sister had a _____ last month. His name's Tom.

3 My little brother's only eight. He's still a _____ .

4 It's great to be a _____ ! I can do lots of things I couldn't do when I was a child.

5 My grandmother's 68, so she's a _____ .

6 My cousin Harry's only 18 months old, so he's a _____ .

c **Vocabulary bank** Complete the sentences with the words in the box.

come of age   getting on
adulthood   look her age
act your age   youth

1 In lots of cultures, when teenagers _come of age_ , they go through a special ceremony.

2 Come on, Sue, _____ _____ ! You're not a child any more.

3 My parents are still very fit, but they are _____ a bit now.

4 My dad always says that school rules were much stricter in his _____ than they are now.

5 _____ is a time when there are lots of responsibilities waiting for you.

6 Your mum looks like your sister! She doesn't _____ at all.

4 Grammar

✱ let / be allowed to

a Write the negatives of the underlined verbs.

1 We're allowed to stay out late.
   We're not allowed to stay out late.

2 I'm allowed to watch TV until 11.30.
   ....

3 You're allowed to cycle here.
   ....

4 The teacher lets us leave early.
   ....

5 Our parents let us play football in the garden.
   ....

6 My brother lets me use his computer.
   ....

b Look at the pictures and complete the sentences with the correct form of *be allowed to*.

① Oh, no! We *'re not allowed to* take photographs here.

② Sorry, sir. You .... park here.

③ OK, off we go, Simon. We .... cycle here.

④ Oh, no! We .... play football here.

⑤ I .... wear trousers at my school.

⑥ Susie, remember that you .... eat or drink inside the library.

c Look at the pictures. Write sentences using (*not*) *let* (*someone*) *do* or (*not*) *be allowed to*.

1 Our father / play football in the garden
   Our father doesn't let us play football in the garden.

2 We / wear jeans to school
   ....
   ....

3 We / run in the school corridor
   ....
   ....

4 My sister / our cat / sleep on her bed
   ....
   ....

5 My parents / me / put posters on my wall
   ....
   ....
   ....

6 Teenagers / go into that club
   ....
   ....
   ....

5 Pronunciation

✱ /əʊ/ and /aʊ/

a ▶ **CD3 T17** Write the words from the box in the correct columns. Then listen and check.

> ~~know~~ ~~now~~ show sound low loud
> round throw shout town house go
> down allowed

/əʊ/	/aʊ/	
know	now	

b ▶ **CD3 T18** Say these sentences. Then listen, check and repeat.

1 Go down to the town centre.
2 We aren't allowed to go out.
3 Don't shout so loudly!
4 Come round to our house.
5 Can you pronounce this sound?

6 Culture in mind

7 Study help

✱ Pronunciation: using a dictionary

a A dictionary can help you pronounce new words, if it provides phonetic symbols. Check the Phonetic symbols list on page 127 of the Student's Book. The letter(s) in bold in the word next to the symbol shows you how to say the sound of each symbol.

b Here are four words from Unit 5. Check their pronunciation in a dictionary. Look at the symbols for the underlined vowels.

allow   tribe
ceremony   bamboo

c Now look up these words in a dictionary. Write their pronunciation using phonetic symbols.

mouse ....

though ....

straight ....

comb ....

Circle the correct option in each sentence. Then check with the quiz on page 44 of the Student's Book.

1 In Brazil you *have* / *are allowed* to vote when you are 16.
2 In the UK you *mustn't* / *are allowed to* get a tattoo when you are under 18.
3 In Arizona, USA, you *can* / *aren't allowed to* get a tattoo at the age of 14.
4 In the UK you *can* / *must* have a bank account at the age of seven.
5 In Japan girls *are* / *aren't* allowed to get married before they are 18.
6 In the USA you *are* / *aren't* allowed to drive a car before you are 21.

Skills in mind

8 Read

a Read this email from Mike to his friend, Amy. Why is he writing to Amy?

_____

_____

_____

Hi Amy!

How are things? You all right? Sorry I haven't replied to your last email, but I've just finished my school exams.

Listen, it's my 16th birthday on 17 June and I'm having a party at my place. Can you come? Hope you can. The party will be great and all my friends are going to be there. Let me know, OK?

See you!

Mike

b Read Amy's reply. Can she go to Mike's party?

_____

Hi Mike

How are you? Hope you're well and your exams were OK!

Thanks a lot for your email – it was good to hear from you. Thanks too for the invitation to your birthday party on the 17th, but we're going on holiday on the 10th and we aren't coming back until the 20th, so I'm afraid there's no way I can go. But I hope you have a really good time and enjoy the party.

I'm really excited about our holiday 'cos we're going to the Bahamas! Can't wait – it's my first time! Lots of sun and swimming, I hope – it'll be great! You won't get a postcard from me of course – you know I'm too lazy! Well, I've got loads of other emails to write so I'll finish here.

Take care and write again soon.

Love

Amy

c Read the email again and write *T* (true) or *F* (false).

1	Amy and her family are going on holiday on 17 June.	F
2	Amy's family will be on holiday for two weeks.	
3	Amy has never been to the Bahamas before.	
4	She wants to do a lot of swimming on holiday.	
5	Mike will get a postcard from Amy.	
6	Amy has to write a lot of other emails.	

WRITING TIP

Informal letters and emails

When you write emails or letters to friends, use an informal style. Study these examples:

- Begin the email/letter with *Hi* (name), or *Hey* (name). (You can also use *Dear* (name) for informal or more formal emails/letters.)

- At the end, write *Love, See you, Write soon* or *Take care* before you write your name.

- In the email/letter, use contractions or short forms. For example: *I'm* (not *I am*), *we're* (not *we are*), *he doesn't* (not *he does not*), etc.

- Show interest in the person you're writing to. Use expressions like: *How are things with you?, Is everything OK?, I hope you're well, Thanks for your (last) email/letter*, etc.

- In very informal writing, sometimes *I* or *you* are left out, when it is clear who the subject is. For example, *Hope you're well*, instead of *I hope you're well*.

Underline examples of informal style in the emails in Exercises 8a and 8b.

9 Write

Imagine you get an email from your English penfriend, inviting you to go and stay with him/her next summer. You can't go because you have planned to spend your summer somewhere else. Write an email to reply to your penfriend. Use Amy's email to help you.

Unit check

1 Fill in the spaces

Complete the text with the words in the box.

| child   baby   get married   let   given   ~~age~~   adult   toddler   pensioner   allowed to |

What's the best _age_ in life? When you are a [1] _____ , life is simple. You're happy if you are [2] _____ enough food and milk and your parents look after you. Then, as a [3] _____ , you learn to walk and begin to discover the world around you. When I was a [4] _____ , my life was great. I loved it when I started school, and learned to read and write. But I wasn't happy when my parents didn't [5] _____ me stay up late or watch TV. Perhaps being an [6] _____ is the best time in life. You're [7] _____ drive a car and vote, and you can [8] _____ , if you find the right person, of course! Or is it best to be a [9] _____ , like my grandfather? He's 72, and he's always happy!

9

2 Choose the correct answers

Circle the correct answer: a, b or c.

1 How many cars _____ every day in the UK?

 a are produced   b produce   c produced

2 Too much energy _____ all over the world.

 a is wasted   b was wasted   c wasting

3 You _____ to sit here.

 a aren't allowed   b isn't allowed   c don't allow

4 His parents _____ go out on week days.

 a let him to   b let him   c are let him

5 _____ your brother let you borrow his trainers?

 a Is   b Does   c Do

6 Some Australian animals _____ in any other country.

 a are not found   b is not found   c don't find

7 These days, cars _____ with the help of computers.

 a is designed   b am designed   c are designed

8 A lot of ice cream _____ every summer.

 a is eaten   b were eaten   c are eaten

9 Susan's parents _____ go to discos.

 a doesn't let her   b don't let her   c allowed to

8

3 Vocabulary

Complete the sentences with the words in the box.

| underage   at least   grounded   youth
childhood   come of age   ~~baby~~
until   act your age |

1 My little brother is still a _baby_ . He can't walk yet.

2 My friends and I are all counting the days until we _____ .

3 She's not a very happy person because she had a difficult _____ .

4 I think in most countries you have to be _____ 18 to drive a car.

5 Stop playing silly games! You're 17, so _____ .

6 Dad says he played football in his _____ .

7 I can't watch that film because I'm only 12 – I'm _____ .

8 Lisa is really tired of being _____ when she stays out late.

9 In the US you're not allowed to drive a car _____ you are 16.

8

How did you do?

Total: **25**

| :) | Very good 20 – 25 | :-| | OK 14 – 19 | :(| Review Unit 5 again 0 – 13 |

6 Have fun!

1 Remember and check

Complete the sentences. Then check with the text on page 46 of the Student's Book.

1 Laughter is good for our _____immune_____ system.

2 When you're stressed, try to _____ a lot.

3 On Red Nose Day, people give money to the 'Comic Relief' _____ .

4 Comic Relief is an organisation that helps people in _____ .

5 They have _____ a lot of money since the first Red Nose Day.

6 The idea of Red Nose Day has _____ to other countries too.

2 Grammar

✱ Present perfect simple

a Tick (✓) the correct sentence in each pair. Put a cross (✗) next to the incorrect sentence.

1 a Jon lives here since 1999. ✗

  b Jon has lived here since 1999. ✓

2 a I've had my bike for two years. ☐

  b I have my bike for two years. ☐

3 a A: How long are you here?
    B: Since eight o'clock. ☐

  b A: How long have you been here?
    B: Since eight o'clock. ☐

4 a I haven't been to school since last week. ☐

  b I haven't been to school for last week. ☐

5 a My mum has worked here for three months. ☐

  b My mum has worked here since three months. ☐

6 a I've seen that film three times. ☐

  b I see that film three times. ☐

b Clown Doctors are clowns dressed up as doctors who help children in hospitals by making them laugh. Complete the text about a Clown Doctor. Use the present perfect simple form of the verbs in brackets.

Dr Helen Marsden talks about Fran Mason, a Clown Doctor

The Clown Doctor _has visited_ (visit) us every month since 2002. Little James Wallace is only five years old, but he [1] _____ (be) in hospital for nearly four months. He laughs so much when the Clown Doctor's here. James [2] _____ (have) three operations since last month, but he's getting much better. James's parents [3] _____ (tell) us that they are sure the Clown Doctor's visits [4] _____ (help) him to get better. Since Fran's last visit, James [5] _____ (ask) me lots of times when she's coming back. We [6] _____ (arrange) for Fran to come back next week, so James is very happy!

c Complete the questions. Use *How long* and the present perfect form of the verbs in brackets.

1 A: Maria and Marco live in Rome.
  B: _How long have they lived_ (live) there?

2 A: I've got a new bike!
  B: Really? _____ (have) it?

3 A: My sister's in Paris.
  B: _____ (be) there?

4 A: My older brother works in that factory.
  B: _____ (work) there?

5 A: Your parents are waiting for you outside.
  B: _____ (be) here?

d Complete the text. Use the present simple or the present perfect form of the verbs in brackets.

Hakan Tasan is 21 and he's from Turkey, but he _lives_ (live) in Dallas, USA. He ¹ _____ (live) there for nearly two years, and he ² _____ (love) it. He ³ _____ (be) a footballer with a Dallas team. He ⁴ _____ (play) in goal, but he ⁵ _____ (not play) any matches for three months, because of a bad foot. 'I ⁶ _____ (want) to play again very soon,' Hakan says. 'Since January, my foot ⁷ _____ (get) much better, so I ⁸ _____ (hope) that next month I'll be back in the team.'

③ Grammar

✱ *for* vs. *since*

a Complete the sentences with *for* and *since*.

1 We've lived in this house   _for_   a long time.
                                    since   1998.

2 My uncle's been here   Saturday.
                                     two days.

3 I haven't eaten anything   yesterday.
                                     24 hours.

4 Our team hasn't won   six months!
                                     last July!

5 Andy hasn't phoned me   last weekend.
                                     a week.

6 I've studied at this school   a very long time!
                                     I was 11.

b Look at the pictures and write sentences. Use the present perfect and *for* or *since*.

1 Tom / be in the library

Tom's been in the library since nine o'clock.

Tom's been in the library for two hours.

2006

2 They / live in this house

_____ .

_____ .

Sunday   Tuesday

3 I / be ill

_____ .

_____ .

2008

4 My aunt / have her car

_____ .

_____ .

2007

5 We / have this computer

_____ .

_____ .

c Complete the sentences. Use the present perfect form of the verbs in brackets and *for* or *since*.

1 Paula's hungry. She
   hasn't eaten (not
   eat) *since* breakfast
   this morning.

2 Tom's hair is too long.
   He _____
   (not cut) it _____
   three years.

3 It's terrible –
   my girlfriend

   _____

   (not phone) me
   _____ Saturday!

5 I'm bored!
   I _____ (not be)
   out _____
   yesterday.

4 Mike and John
   aren't happy. They

   _____

   (not play) football
   _____ two weeks.

6 I hope the film's good.
   I _____
   (not see) a good film
   _____ a long time.

d Write six true sentences about you / your family / your friends. Use the present perfect and *for* or *since*.

I've lived in this town since I was three years old.   *Carlo and I have been friends for three years.*

1 I / live / this town _____ .
2 I / have / (my computer / my bicycle / my dog / my cat) _____ .
3 I / be / friends with _____ .
4 _____ .
5 _____ .
6 _____ .

④ Pronunciation

✱ have, has and for

a ▶ CD3 T19 Read the sentences and <u>underline</u> the words you think are stressed. Then listen, check and repeat. Pay special attention to the pronunciation of *has* and *have*.

1 <u>Where</u> have you <u>been</u>?
2 How long has he been there?
3 My parents have bought a new car.
4 James has gone home.

b ▶ CD3 T20 Now read these sentences. <u>Underline</u> the words you think are stressed. Then listen, check and repeat. Pay special attention to the pronunciation of *for*.

1 He's <u>been</u> here for <u>ages</u>.
2 We've lived here for a long time.
3 I've had this bike for three months.
4 We haven't eaten for two hours.

5 Vocabulary

✱ Verb and noun pairs

a Complete the sentences. Use the correct form of *have* or *make*.

1 Last night's party was great! We really _had_ fun.

2 It's my birthday next Saturday, so don't _____ any plans.

3 I haven't done very well – I _____ four mistakes!

4 The film was very funny. We really _____ a good laugh!

5 I fell off my bike and my friends _____ fun of me.

6 I hope you enjoy the party – _____ a good time!

6 Everyday English

Complete the dialogue. Use the expressions in the box.

> in other words   What's the point of
> come on   as long as
> ~~Tell me about it~~   Know what

Sharon: Hi Ben. It's me – Sharon. Have you finished your homework?

Ben: Yes – it was really hard, though!

Sharon: _Tell me about it_ ! I worked for three hours! So, what are you doing?

Ben: I'm playing my new computer game.

Sharon: Oh, Ben! [1]_____ playing computer games? They're a waste of time.

Ben: No, they aren't. You can learn a lot from a computer game, [2]_____ you choose the right one.

Sharon: Oh, [3]_____ ! You aren't playing the game because it's educational!

Ben: No, you're right. I'm playing it because it's fun.

Sharon: Ah! So, [4]_____ , it's a game first and a learning thing second!

Ben: Oh, Sharon. [5]_____ ? I need to relax. So I'm going back to my game!

b

Vocabulary bank Complete the text. Use the correct form of *have*, *make* or *take*.

Dear Annie,

I [1]_have_ a problem. Next Friday, I have to [2]_____ my driving test. I'm really nervous because last week I [3]_____ an accident during my driving lesson. Until then, I [4]_____ a lot of progress, but now I think I should [5]_____ a break and cancel the test. What should I do? I have to [6]_____ a decision today!

Thanks, Emma

7 Study help

✱ How to learn English tenses

a You may find some English tenses like the present perfect difficult. Read these ideas to help you.

- Underline examples of the present perfect in the Student's Book and the Workbook. Do the same with any songs in English that you know.

- When you read, find examples of the present perfect. Think about **why** it is used.

- When you listen to your teacher (or other English speakers), listen for examples of the present perfect and think about why he/she has used it.

- Learn from your mistakes! It's OK to make mistakes and it's a normal part of learning.

b Read the paragraph below. Underline examples of the present perfect.

Birmingham student wins trip to California

Michael Thompson, a student from Birmingham, has won the first prize in a competition for student computer programmers. Michael is 19 and studied at St John's High School, Portsmouth, before going to Aston University, Birmingham. He has been interested in computing since he was 12, and has already written several pieces of software. Michael entered the competition when Professor Samuels, who has been his teacher for a year, suggested that he could do well.

c Look at the notes on the present perfect on page 93.

Skills in mind

How to answer multiple choice questions

- Read the whole text first, before you look at the questions and options. Use the title and picture(s) to help you understand the whole text. Look at the title and picture of the text on this page. What do you think the text is about?

- Read each question and the options carefully. <u>Underline</u> the most important (key) words in each question. Look at **question 1**. The key words are *Hunter Adams*, *went*, *Virginia*, *because*. Find the part of the text that has the answer. The word *Virginia* will help you because it starts with a capital *V*.

- Read that part of the text carefully again.

- Usually there is at least one option that is clearly wrong because there is no information about it at all in that part of the text. In **question 1**, *a* is clearly wrong because at the start of the second paragraph it says that Adams went to Virginia after he left hospital.

- Remember: you don't have to understand **everything** in the text. The exercise asks you to find the answers to the questions, not to understand all the words in the text.

8 Read

Read the text and (circle) the correct answer: a, b or c.

Hunter 'Patch' Adams

When he was a teenager, Hunter Adams was very unhappy, and he spent many years in the 1960s and 1970s in a special hospital for people with mental health problems.

When he left hospital, Adams decided to become a doctor, so he went to medical school in Virginia, USA. But when he was there, he did things in a different way. For example, he didn't like the doctors' white coats, so he wore shirts with flowers on them when he visited his patients, and he tried to make them laugh. The doctors at the medical school didn't like Adams very much because he was too different.

But Adams believed that people in hospital need more than medicine. He saw unhappy and lonely people, and he tried to help them as patients, but as people too. He spent a lot of time with children in the hospital, and often put a special red nose on his face to look like a clown and to make the children laugh.

When he finished medical school and became a doctor, Adams opened his own hospital, called 'The Gesundheit Institute', together with some other doctors. They wanted it to be a place with a different way of working with sick people.

Hunter Adams became famous during the 1980s, and in 1998, Universal Pictures made a film about his life. It was very successful. In the film (called Patch Adams), Robin Williams played Adams. Williams said, 'Hunter is a really warm person, who believes that patients need a doctor who's a friend. I enjoyed playing him.'

1 Hunter Adams went to Virginia because …
   a   he had mental health problems.
   b   he wanted to be a doctor.
   c   he did things differently.

2 Adams wore shirts with flowers on them because …
   a   he didn't want to wear a white coat.
   b   the doctors didn't like him.
   c   it made the patients laugh.

3 Adams thought that many people in hospital …
   a   didn't need medicine.
   b   were unhappy and lonely.
   c   weren't nice people.

4 Adams started The Gesundheit Institute …
   a   with other doctors.
   b   on his own.
   c   with different sick people.

5 Universal Pictures made a film about Hunter Adams because …
   a   his hospital was very successful.
   b   Robin Williams was his friend.
   c   he was a famous person.

Unit check

1 Fill in the spaces

Complete the text with the words in the box.

| funny faces | makes fun | since | made fools | ~~good laugh~~ | time | for | make me | haven't | fun |

I love having a _good laugh_ and I like people who [1] _____ laugh. For example, my best friend, Sarah. I've known her [2] _____ nine years and she's really great. She loves telling jokes, but she never [3] _____ of other people. At the weekend we usually have a lot of [4] _____ . We often go to the park and have a cola and a good [5] _____ together. But one Sunday, a few weeks ago, we [6] _____ of ourselves! We were sitting under a tree in the park, making [7] _____ for about half an hour. Then we saw that two boys from my class were watching us! We [8] _____ been to the park [9] _____ that Sunday!

9

2 Choose the correct answers

(Circle) the correct answer: a, b or c.

1 Gerry is nice. He _____ in my class since Christmas.
   a (has been) b is c was

2 How long _____ this bike?
   a you had b have you c have you had

3 I'm going to see my cousin next week. We _____ for two years.
   a don't meet b haven't met c didn't meet

4 My parents _____ for 15 years.
   a have been married b have married c are married

5 David _____ with us since the summer.
   a has been b is c was

6 I'm sorry I _____ since we last spoke. I've been so busy!
   a didn't phone b haven't phoned c don't phone

7 You must be hungry. You _____ since last night.
   a haven't eaten b didn't eat c hasn't eaten

8 My sister has hated tomato soup _____ she was a child.
   a for b when c since

9 Carol and I _____ penfriends for three years.
   a have been b are c been

8

3 Vocabulary

Complete the sentences. Use the correct form of *make* or *take*.

1 When you phoned we _were making_ dinner.

2 I think we need to _____ a plan before we start.

3 We aren't in a hurry, so let's _____ our time and enjoy the journey.

4 When I heard what he said, it _____ me smile.

5 My grandfather _____ his driving test when he was 55!

6 Learning the guitar was difficult at first, but now I'm _____ a lot of progress.

7 If you have a better idea, please feel free to _____ a suggestion!

8 He's interested in other people and _____ friends easily.

9 My sister _____ an interest in her friends. They all like her.

8

How did you do?

Total: **25**

| :) Very good 20 – 25 | :\| OK 14 – 19 | :(Review Unit 6 again 0 – 13 |

7 Disaster!

1 Remember and check

Match the two parts of the sentences. Then check with Exercise 1d on page 55 of the Student's Book.

1 In 2005 New Orleans was hit by
2 Many people left the city, but
3 More than seven thousand were
4 The city was badly damaged – about
5 Many people lost everything they had

a 1,500 people were killed.
b and the damage was 90 billion dollars.
c a terrible Hurricane named Katrina.
d rescued by the police and firefighters.
e 80% of the city was flooded.

2 Grammar

✳ Past simple passive

a Complete the sentences with the past participle form of the verbs in the box.

speak   lose   give   ~~see~~   send   break

1 The film *Gladiator* was __seen__ by more than 100 million people.
2 There was a terrible storm last night. Four windows were _____ in our house.
3 The criminals were caught, and they were _____ to prison.
4 The French language was _____ by many people in England after 1066.
5 Thousands of umbrellas were _____ on London Underground trains last year.
6 My sister and I were _____ a DVD player for Christmas.

b Circle the correct words.

1 Martin Luther King won / was won the Nobel Peace prize in 1964.
2 In 1968, King killed / was killed in Memphis, USA.
3 My bicycle stole / was stolen last week.
4 Luckily, it found / was found again two days later.
5 Television didn't invent / wasn't invented until 1946.
6 Twenty years later, the first colour TVs sold / were sold.

c Complete the text with the present simple passive or past simple passive form of the verbs in brackets.

Earthquakes happen in Los Angeles very often. The city __was built__ (build) on top of the San Andreas Fault, one of the worst places in the world for earthquakes. Every year many windows [1] _____ (break) and many houses [2] _____ (damage) by small earthquakes.

In 1994, the city [3] _____ (hit) by a really bad earthquake which measured 6.6 on the Richter scale. Many buildings [4] _____ (damage) by fire; a motorway [5] _____ (destroy) by the earthquake; and many people [6] _____ (kill) in their cars. After that earthquake, new building laws [7] _____ (introduce) and today all new houses in the Los Angeles area [8] _____ (build) to survive earthquakes.

d Rewrite the sentences. Use the past simple passive.

1 They built a new road near my house.

A new road was built near my house.

2 They killed 100,000 soldiers in the war.

_____ .

3 Someone left the door open last night.

_____ .

4 They printed all the books on time.

_____ .

5 They closed the main railway station yesterday.

_____ .

6 Someone stole all my money.

_____ .

7 The hotel porter took my suitcase to my room.

_____ .

e Complete the text. Use the past simple or past simple passive form of the verbs in brackets.

SUMATRA

Krakatoa □

JAVA

Indian Ocean

INDONESIA has many volcanoes. One of the most famous is Krakatoa, a small island volcano in the sea between Java and Sumatra. On the night of 26 August 1883, Krakatoa *erupted* (erupt). Here are some facts about the eruption:

1 Before the eruption, Krakatoa was an island of about 47 km², and people ¹_____ (live) there. After the eruption, it was only 16 km², and now no one can live there.

2 Before 1883, Krakatoa was one island, but after the eruption, a smaller island ²_____ (appear). It ³_____ (push) out of the sea by the force of the explosion. The second island ⁴_____ (give) the name Anak Krakatoa, which means 'child of Krakatoa' in Indonesian.

3 Thousands of people ⁵_____ (kill), but we don't know exactly how many.

4 There was also an earthquake under the sea. It ⁶_____ (produce) by a tsunami wave that was almost 15 m high. The wave ⁷_____ (travel) nearly 13,000 km!

5 The explosion ⁸_____ (make) a very loud noise – it ⁹_____ (hear) by people in Australia!

6 Millions of tonnes of volcanic dust ¹⁰_____ (throw) into the atmosphere, and the result was some of the most beautiful sunsets that have ever been seen.

7 In 1927, Krakatoa ¹¹_____ (produce) some small eruptions. Since then, the island has been quiet. But who knows when the next eruption will be?

3 Pronunciation

✱ 'Silent' letters

▶ **CD3 T21** Read the sentences and <u>underline</u> the letters that are not pronounced. Then listen, check and repeat.

1 She <u>k</u>nows the an<u>sw</u>er.
2 I <u>w</u>rote the <u>w</u>rong thing.
3 Listen to the answers.
4 They're climbing up a tall building.
5 They built a castle in the mountains.

4 Vocabulary

✱ Disasters

a Fill in the crossword.

1 $500 million of *damage* was caused by a tsunami in Hawaii in 1960.
2 Katrina was the worst ... to hit the USA for a very long time.
3 A terrible ... hit Mexico City in 1985.
4 ... can happen when rivers have too much water in them.
5 Many people worked for days to ... the victims from the earthquake.
6 Mount Etna is a famous ... in Italy.
7 A ... bomb makes a cloud shaped like a mushroom.
8 1,500 people in New Orleans were ... in 2005 by Katrina.
9 A ... is a small insect that can cause terrible damage to farms and people.
10 A ... is a giant wave, often caused by an underwater earthquake.
11 Every time there is a natural disaster, a lot of money is ... .

b [Vocabulary bank] Complete the sentences with the words in the box.

> collapse   cracked   ~~set fire~~   catch fire
> starving   on fire   homeless   put out

1 Someone _set fire_ to the factory last night.
2 Look at that smoke! I think the building over there is _____ .
3 Hundreds of houses were destroyed, and many people were _____ .
4 It's dangerous to smoke in bed, because the bed might _____ .
5 We got lots of water to _____ the fire.
6 There isn't enough food, so a lot of people are _____ .
7 That house is very old – I think it's going to _____ soon.
8 Sorry – I dropped the glass. It isn't broken, but it's _____ .

5 Grammar

✱ *a/an, the* or *zero article*

a Complete the sentences with *a* or *an*.

1 I got ___*a*___ bicycle for Christmas.
2 Can I have _____ orange, please?
3 It's raining. Take _____ umbrella with you.
4 We've got _____ examination next week.
5 We stayed in _____ hotel in Rome.
6 Is this _____ apple or _____ pear?

b Complete the paragraph with *a*, *the* or [–] (no article).

> This story is about – robbers. I was in bed last [1] _____ night when I heard [2] _____ strange noise. I got up and went to my window. [3] _____ noise was coming from our neighbours' garden. I saw two men. They were putting [4] _____ ladder against the wall of the house next door. I didn't know who [5] _____ men were, so I called [6] _____ police.

6 Culture in mind

a Write *T* (true) or *F* (false). Then check with the text on page 58 in the Student's Book.

1 The Tuvalu islands in the South Pacific are in danger because of climate change. `T`

2 Geographically speaking, Tuvalu is the smallest country in the world. ☐

3 In the southern summer, the group of islands gets severe hurricanes and rough seas. ☐

4 One day, the Tuvaluans will have to leave their islands because there won't be enough food any more. ☐

5 New Zealand has agreed to take in 9,000 immigrants per year from Tuvalu. ☐

6 The Australian government won't accept immigrants from Tuvalu. ☐

7 It is not clear where the people of Tuvalu will go when they can't live on their islands any more. ☐

b Complete the sentences with the words in the box. Put the words into their correct form where necessary.

> threaten   reduce   rising   tiny   source
> ~~uninhabitable~~   refuse   rough

1 Tuvalu might become __*uninhabitable*__ because of climate change.

2 Geographically speaking, Tuvalu is a _____ country.

3 Tuvalu is frequently hit by hurricanes, which cause storms and _____ seas.

4 Frequent hurricanes have started to _____ life in Tuvalu.

5 _____ sea levels have increased the level of salt in the ground water.

6 Ground water is the only _____ of fresh water for people and farm animals.

7 The government has started a programme to _____ Tuvalu's emission of greenhouse gases.

8 The Australian government has _____ to take in Tuvaluan immigrants.

7 Study help

✱ Speaking: how to improve your fluency

In many tests and examinations, you will often have to speak English. Many students think that the **only** important thing is not to make any mistakes, but this is not true! You are tested on your ability to communicate successfully, and fluency is an important part of communication.

Here are some ideas to help you speak fluently:

- Keep calm, and give yourself time to think. Don't rush!
- Think about the message you want to communicate, not only about the grammar.
- If you make a mistake, don't worry! It's normal to make mistakes, so don't stop or panic.
- If you can't remember how to say a word in English, don't stop or panic! Try to explain the word if you can. For example, if you can't remember the word *kitchen*, say, 'The room in the house where I cook'.
- It's OK to pause or stop occasionally if you need to think about how to say something. But try not to pause too many times or for too long.
- If you are asked a question, try not to give too many short answers. For example, if the other person asks, 'Have you got any brothers or sisters?' don't just say, 'Yes, I have' or 'No, I haven't'. Say, for example, 'Yes, I've got a sister called Sabrina, and she's 12, and a brother called Marco. He's 11.'

Choose one of the topics below. Think about it for one minute, and then try to talk about it for one minute without stopping. It's better if you can do this with a friend or someone in your family.

- my favourite film star
- my house
- my best friend
- my favourite shops
- the things I like doing in my free time

Skills in mind

Listening for specific information

It's important to look carefully at the task before the listening starts. You are usually given time to do this.

- Read each question very carefully. What kind of information does the question ask you to find? A date? A time? A name? A place?

- You don't need to understand *everything* in the recording. Look at the questions and listen carefully for the answers.

- Look at the listening exercise on this page. What kind of information do you need to answer questions 2–5? You will hear the names of cities and other places in the countries. Do you need to listen for these?

8 Listen

✱ Great earthquakes in history

▶ **CD3 T22** Listen to an interview about important earthquakes in history. Listen and put the information in the correct places in the table.

Japan	Ecuador	China	~~Sicily (Italy)~~	Portugal
~~1693~~	1797	1755	1710	1556
80,000	800,000	~~60,000~~	200,000	40,000

	Country	Year	Number of people killed
1	*Sicily (Italy)*	*1693*	*60,000*
2			
3			
4			
5			

9 Read

a Look at the picture and the title of the text. Can you guess what the story is about? Read the text quickly and answer the questions.

1 What's the man's name?
   The man's name is Harry Truman.

2 How old was he when he died?
   ....

3 Where did he live
   ....

4 How did he die? ....

b Read the text again and answer the questions.

1 Why did Harry stay on the mountain, do you think?
   ....
   ....

2 Was a helicopter sent to rescue Harry? Why (not), do you think?
   ....
   ....

HE DIDN'T WANT TO LEAVE

Harry Truman died on 18 May 1980 when he was 84 years old. He lived in a small house on Mount St Helens, in Washington State, USA. Harry went to live there in 1926. In 1975 his wife died and for the next five years, Harry lived alone.

In April 1980 scientists in the USA realised that the Mount St Helens volcano was going to erupt. Hundreds of families from many towns around the mountain moved away, but not Harry. In the weeks before the volcano erupted, newspaper reporters came to Harry's house and asked him why he wasn't leaving. Harry told them the mountain was his home, and said that he planned to stay there.

'He always said that the mountain was his friend,' said one of Harry's friends. 'I knew he was going to die, and I told him, but he refused to leave his home.'

But George Barker, a local policeman, said, 'I think old Harry liked the stories about him. It made him famous, and he enjoyed that. But I think Harry believed that at the last moment, the newspapers would send a helicopter to take him off the mountain.'

But when the mountain exploded, no helicopter came and the red-hot lava hit Spirit Lake at 200 km/h. The lake, Harry and his house all disappeared under the volcanic rock. No one ever saw Harry again.

Unit check

1 Fill in the spaces

Complete the text with the words in the box.

> hurricanes   destroy   ~~disasters~~   the   volcano   floods   lose   tsunami   earthquakes   killed

Disasters happen all the time, and in many parts of the world. For example, sometimes people on islands in the South Sea are ¹_____ by ²_____ .

In California, there are lots of ³_____ (the one in San Francisco in 1906 was very strong). An earthquake under ⁴_____ sea can cause a ⁵_____ , a giant wave that can kill or injure thousands of people.

In some countries, when it rains heavily, there are ⁶_____ . Many people ⁷_____ their homes.

And lastly, when a ⁸_____ like Vesuvius or Krakatoa erupts, it can easily ⁹_____ everything nearby.

9

2 Choose the correct answers

(Circle) the correct answer: a, b or c.

1 That house _____ last month.

   a sold   b is sold   c (was sold)

2 My dad's car keys _____ yesterday.

   a are stolen   b was stolen   c were stolen

3 That tower _____ hundreds of years ago.

   a were built   b is built   c was built

4 About 2,000 years ago, the city of Pompeii _____ by a volcano.

   a was destroyed   b is destroyed
   c were destroyed

5 On Sunday I saw _____ interesting film about tsunamis.

   a a   b an   c the

6 My mother rides a motorbike. It's _____ old Kawasaki.

   a a   b the   c an

7 I got _____ nice new photo album for my birthday this year.

   a a   b an   c the

8 When _____ the Tower of London built?

   a was built   b was   c is

9 In the flood last month, all the houses by the river _____ .

   a destroying   b are destroyed
   c were destroyed

8

3 Vocabulary

<u>Underline</u> the correct word in each sentence.

- All the world's countries should work together to ¹ _increase / reduce / rise_ their ² _emission / situation / immigration_ of greenhouse gases.
- Fishermen can't get to their ³ _course / source / programme_ of income because of the ⁴ _tiny / uninhabitable / rough_ seas.
- When New Orleans was ⁵ _built / hurt / hit_ by hurricane Katrina, lots of houses were badly ⁶ _rescued / upset / damaged_.

- The city of Pompeii was completely ⁷ _disaster / flooded / destroyed_ by a volcano more than two thousand years ago.
- Hurricane Katrina was one of the biggest ⁸ _floods / damage / disasters_ in American history.
- The ⁹ _estimate / damage / research_ to the city cost 90 billion dollars.

8

How did you do?

Total: 25

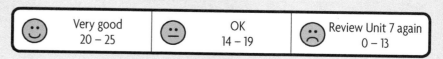

| | Very good 20 – 25 | | OK 14 – 19 | | Review Unit 7 again 0 – 13 |

8 Ways of living

1 Remember and check

Read part of the text about the historic caves in Andalusia. Put the lines in the correct order. Then check your answers with the text on page 60 of the Student's Book.

- [ ] to find everything you need – electricity, phone, hot water. Some caves
- [ ] primitive. Well, you haven't seen these caves. A
- [1] You probably think caves are
- [ ] have a Jacuzzi or a swimming pool.
- [ ] a small country cottage to a luxurious cave
- [ ] even have a broadband connection and others
- [ ] hotel. Come and enjoy the peaceful environment. You'll be surprised
- [ ] cave house in Andalusia can be anything from

2 Grammar

✳ too much/many, not enough

a Use *too much* or *too many* to match the two parts of the sentences.

~~We spent~~		tests at school.
Be quiet, please! There's		~~money today!~~
I think we get	too much	sugar in my coffee.
Jack was sick because he ate	too many	noise in here.
I put		ice cream yesterday.
You always ask me		questions!

1 *We spent too much money today!* _____
2 _____
   _____ .
3 _____
   _____ .
4 _____
   _____ .
5 _____
   _____ .
6 _____
   _____ .

b Complete the sentences with *too much*, *too many* or *not (n't) enough*.

1 There were _too many_ people and there were _n't enough_ chairs for everybody.

There are 50 questions in the test. You have 15 minutes to answer them all.

2 The test was awful! There were _____ questions and there was _____ time to answer them all.

!!!

3 I think I've made _____ food, and there are _____ drinks.

4 I've got _____ CDs and there is _____ space for them all!

5 The party was awful! There were _____ girls and there were _____ boys!

3 Pronunciation

✱ Sound and spelling: -ou

a ▶ **CD3 T23** Write the words in the lists. Then listen, check and repeat.

~~enough~~ out famous could

/aʊ/	/ʌ/	/ʊ/	/ə/
	enough		

b ▶ **CD3 T24** Say the sentences. Then listen and check.

1 We've got a big house.
2 Could I have a glass of water?
3 Those dogs are dangerous.
4 This exercise is really tough.

4 Vocabulary

✱ Homes

a Look at the picture and write the words in the box in the correct places.

fence ~~window~~ door garden garage chimney TV aerial

b Fill in the word puzzle. What's the mystery word? _____

1 They're building a new *block* of flats in our street.
2 My best friend lives on a ... estate.
3 There's a ... on the roof of our house.
4 There are some beautiful flowers in our ... .
5 They haven't got a lift, so we'll have to walk up the ... .
6 My bedroom's on the second ... of our house.
7 My grandparents live in a small ... in the country.
8 We can see the park from our living room ... .

			1	b	l	o	c	k	
		2			s				
3						y			
	4							n	
	5					s			
	6				o				
	7			t					
	8						o		

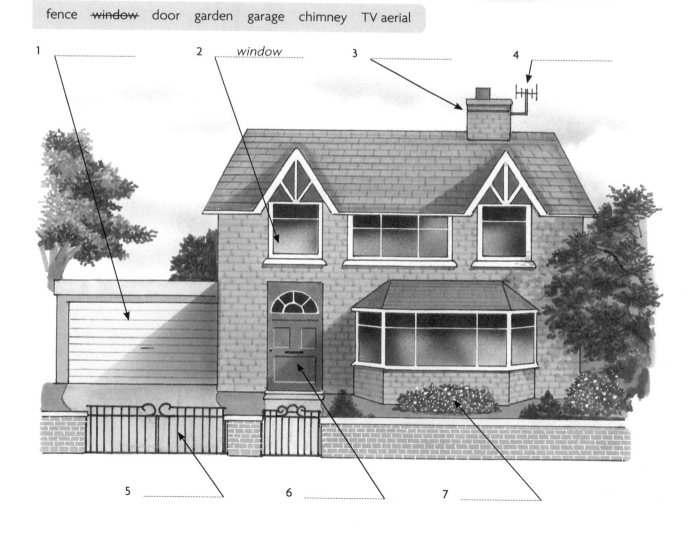

1 _____
2 *window*
3 _____
4 _____
5 _____
6 _____
7 _____

roof   central heating   share   balcony   basement   ~~air conditioning~~   move house   attic

Some friends of ours have got a cottage by the sea. It's a bit old and doesn't have any __*air conditioning*__ or [1] _____ (so it's cold in winter!), but it's a great place for weekends. When you go down into the [2] _____ , there are boxes full of old books. I sometimes choose a book, then I climb the ladder all the way up to the [3] _____ and start reading. It's only a problem when it rains — the [4] _____ has got a few holes! The house has got a [5] _____ , too, overlooking the sea. Unfortunately, my parents want to [6] _____ and we're going to live in another city. It's far away so we won't be able to visit the cottage by the sea so often. And in our new place I'll have to [7] _____ a room with my brother! :-(

5 Grammar

✱ *will* vs. *be going to*

a Underline the correct options. Then check with the dialogue on page 63 of the Student's Book.

> Jake is going to [1] <u>China</u> / *India*. He's going to visit a place called [2] *Beijing / Qinghai*, where there are lots of Tibetan people. He's also going to visit some Tibetan people in their [3] *tents / caravans*. Jake will pack some [4] *socks / warm clothes* because it's cold there. When he's there, he'll [5] *phone Angie / send Angie a postcard* if he can.

b Write *A* if the sentence is a decision made at the moment of speaking, or *B* if it's a decision made before the moment of speaking.

1   I'm bored! I think I'll phone Alison.   *A*

2   We're going to have a party next weekend.   *B*

3   Our teacher says he's going to give us a test next week.   ☐

4   I'm hungry. I think I'll make a sandwich.   ☐

5   You haven't got any money? Don't worry — I'll lend you some.   ☐

6   It's Steve's birthday next week and I'm going to buy him a great present!   ☐

7   There's a test next Monday, so I'm going to study over the weekend.   ☐

8   It's very cold in here, isn't it? I'll close the window.   ☐

c Match the sentences with the pictures. Write 1–6 in the boxes.

1   ~~I'll answer it.~~

2   I'll carry it for you.

3   I'm going to New York next month.

4   I'm going to lose weight this year.

5   My dad's going to buy a new one next week.

6   Don't cry — I'll buy you another one.

A   1 January   200X

B   NEW YORK 10 December

C   ☐ 1

D ☐

E ☐

F ☐

d (Circle) the correct words.

1   I want to visit Paris next year, so I (*'m going to*) / *'ll* learn French next term.

2   There aren't any good films on TV tonight, so I think I *'m going to* / *'ll* watch the football.

3   My computer's old, so my dad *'s going to* / *'ll* buy me a new one for my birthday.

4   My sister and I have planned our holiday. We *'re going to* / *'ll* visit our cousin in Scotland.

5   I haven't spoken to John for a long time. I think I *'m going to* / *'ll* phone him now.

6   What can I get Jane for her birthday? I know — I *'m going to* / *'ll* take her to the cinema.

7   I don't want to do this homework now. I think I *'m going to* / *'ll* do it tomorrow instead.

6 Everyday English

a Put the words in the correct order.

1 else you Anything need ?   _Anything else you need?_

2 say If so you   ....

3 you up It's to   ....

4 point There's arguing in no   ....

5 it wrong with nothing There's   ....

6 place all They're over the   ....

b Complete the dialogues. Use the expressions from Exercise 6a.

1 A: OK – you've got skis and boots and poles and warm clothes.
   Anything else you need?
   B: No, I don't think so, thanks.

2 A: This food doesn't look very good. Is it OK to eat?
   B: Yes, it's fine, you can eat it.
   ....

3 A: Look at all these books on the floor.
   B: I know. ....
   Let's tidy them up.

4 A: But Dad – I don't want to go to Aunt Sally's house tomorrow. It's boring!
   B: Listen, Mike. You're coming with us, and that's that. OK? ....

5 A: What shall we have for lunch? Pizza or salad?
   B: .... I like them both.

6 A: That new boy, Dan – he's really good-looking!
   B: .... – but I don't think he's very special.

7 Study help

✳ Vocabulary: nouns and verbs

a Many nouns don't change form when used as verbs. Study these examples:

- I <u>promise</u> I'll bring the book back tomorrow. (verb)
- I'll ring you next week – that's a <u>promise</u>! (noun)

b Look at the <u>underlined</u> words in sentences 1–10 and write *V* (verb) or *N* (noun).

1   We're going to <u>move</u> next month. | V |

2   Come on, Steve. It's your <u>move</u>. | N |

3   Are you thirsty? I'll get you some <u>water</u>. | |

4   We're going to <u>water</u> the plants now. | |

5   My dad's going to <u>work</u> in Paris next week. | |

6   Sorry, I'm busy. I've got too much <u>work</u> to do. | |

7   I'm going to clear my desk – there's too much <u>paper</u> on it. | |

8   I'm going to <u>paper</u> the walls in my bedroom next week. | |

9   Would you like a <u>drink</u>? | |

10 I usually <u>drink</u> water in the morning. | |

8 Read

Read this advertisement for a house and write
T (true) or *F* (false).

1 The house is in the town centre. `F`

2 Schools are a long way from the house. ☐

3 The house is well-decorated. ☐

4 There are seven rooms in the house. ☐

5 The house has a garden at the back. ☐

6 You can try to buy this house for less
than £350,000. ☐

7 If you want to visit the house, you have
to phone first. ☐

City house in excellent location

This detached home was built in the early
1980s and is located in a quiet residential
street not far from the town centre. Schools,
transport and many local services are all in
the close vicinity. The house has been well
maintained by the original owners, and is
decorated to a very high standard.

The accommodation comprises a spacious
living room with an open fire place, separate
dining room, a large, well-equipped and
modern kitchen, three ample bedrooms
(one en suite) and a further bathroom. There
is also a garden with lawns and flower beds
at the front of the premises, and a garage
with utility area and space for two average-
sized cars. All carpets, cupboards and
kitchen fittings are included in the price.

The asking price is £350,000
– no offers below this price will be accepted.

Visits by telephone appointment.

READING TIP

Reading for detailed information

Sometimes you need to read part of a
text very carefully to answer a question
correctly.

● When you read a question, always
go to the place in the text where
you can find the answer. Read the
sentence(s) there two or three times,
and compare what you read with the
question. The answer can sometimes
depend on just one or two words.

● Look at the reading text in Exercise 8,
and the *true/false* questions.

— Look at question 1. Which sentence
in the text will tell you the answer?
(The first sentence)

— Which part of the sentence refers
to the town centre? (The last part)

— What are the three words before
the town centre? (*not far from*)

— Are there any other words in the
sentence which help you find the
answer? (*quiet, street*)

— Is question 1 true or false? (False)

Do the same for the other six questions.

9 Write

Write a description of the house or flat
where you live. Include the following
information:

● how old your house/flat is

● the location (is it in the centre, in a
suburb, in a village?)

● the services near your house/flat
(schools, shops, cinemas, a park?)

● how many rooms your house/flat has
got, and a short description of each room

● what kind of decoration the rooms have
got (the colours, carpets, wallpaper?)

● what you like most about your house/
flat

Unit check

1 Fill in the spaces

Complete the text with the words in the box.

| floor   detached   too much   ~~flats~~   garage   enough   garden   semi-detached   chimney   housing |

My dad says that he wants us to move into a block of _flats_ ! But I don't want to move – I like our nice
¹ _____ house! We've got a ² _____ for the car and my brother and I can play in the
³ _____ here too. I know it's a bit noisy here, because there's ⁴ _____ traffic on our street, but
who wants to live in a flat? My friend lives in a flat and it's awful! I don't think it's nice to have everything
on one ⁵ _____ , and they can't have a fire, because there's no ⁶ _____ ! I don't want to live on
a ⁷ _____ estate either because all the houses look the same. I'd really like to live in a big
⁸ _____ house in the country, so I can make as much noise as I like – but my dad says we haven't
got ⁹ _____ money!

[9]

2 Choose the correct answers

(Circle) the correct answer: a, b or c.

1 I can't hear you. There's _____ noise.

   a (too much)   b too many   c not enough

2 I have _____ emails to write.

   a too much   b too many   c not enough

3 We haven't got _____ food for everybody.

   a enough   b too much   c too many

4 A: I'm so busy!

   B: Don't worry. _____ help you.

   a I'm going to   b I'll   c I

5 On Saturday we _____ see the Kings of Leon in concert.

   a go to   b 're going to   c will

6 They _____ the USA for three weeks this summer.

   a 're going to   b 'll go to   c go to

7 I don't think there _____ be cars in the future.

   a won't   b aren't going to   c will

8 I didn't finish my project because there wasn't _____
   information on the Internet.

   a too many   b enough   c too much

9 Next week we _____ U2 live – we've bought the tickets!

   a 're going to see   b will see   c see

[8]

3 Vocabulary

Put the letters in the correct order to make words. Write the word(s) next to the sentence.

1 The fire place doesn't work. I think we need to have the _chimney_ repaired. (emynhic)

2 Don't open the _____ .
   There's a dog in the garden! (tage)

3 My grandparents like to sit on the _____ of their flat in the summer. (yonclab)

4 It must be great to live in a _____ . (rvncaaa)

5 They're building some new _____ in our street. (lugaoswnb)

6 These _____ houses were built 25 years ago. (daceerrt)

7 I had to climb on the roof to fix the TV _____ . (liarea)

8 We are going to change one room in the _____ to a gym. (enmasbet)

9 I found this book in a box in our [8] _____ . (catit)

How did you do?

Total: [25]

| 😊 Very good 20 – 25 | 😐 OK 14 – 19 | 🙁 Review Unit 8 again 0 – 13 |

9 Your mind

1 Remember and check

(Circle) the correct information in each sentence. Then check your answers with the text on page 68 of the Student's Book.

1   Your brain is like a muscle – (use) / lose it or use / (lose) it.

2   The brain makes up *2 / 20* per cent of our total body weight and needs *2 / 20* per cent of the oxygen that our body takes in.

3   *No one / Everyone* can remember *everything / nothing*, but *no one / everyone* can learn how to improve their memory.

4   When you want to remember *something / somebody*, tell *something / somebody* about it.

5   It's better to study *a lot / a small amount* of material for *a lot / a small amount* of time than the other way round.

2 Grammar

✱ Determiners (*everyone, no one, someone*, etc.)

a (Circle) the correct words.

1   This is a great DVD. I think (*everyone*) / *all of them* should buy it.

2   There were lots of questions. *Some of them / All of them* were easy, but the others were difficult.

3   We always go to the same place! Can't we go *everywhere / somewhere* different tonight?

4   I've travelled to lots of countries, but *somewhere / nowhere* is as beautiful as my country.

5   I don't know what to buy Jim for his birthday. He's got *everything / everyone*!

6   You've eaten all the food! There's *nothing / something* left!

7   He's a really horrible person – *no one / everyone* likes him.

8   I've got five brothers and sisters and *no one / none of them* likes music!

b Look at the pictures and complete the sentences. Use determiners (*everyone, no one, someone*, etc).

1   I invited lots of people to my party, but ___no one___ came!

2   I've got a lot of T-shirts and _____ are black!

3   I've looked _____, but I just can't find my camera!

4   I got the wrong number. _____ answered, but I didn't know who it was.

5   I've got lots of friends at school, but _____ are as tall as me.

6   The bus was full, and there was _____ to sit.

3 Vocabulary

✱ Thinking

a Fill in the word puzzle.

1	R
2	E
3	A
4	L
5	I
6	S
7	E

1 He looked very different – I didn't ... him!
2 I didn't know the answers, so I had to ... .
3 I can't ... what it's like to walk on the moon!
4 That's not true! I don't ... you.
5 I ... it's fun to learn another language.
6 It's late, so I ... I should go to bed.
7 I was very tired, so I couldn't ... on my work.

b Complete the sentences with the words in the box.

naturalistic   mathematical   intrapersonal   visual   ~~body~~   verbal   interpersonal   musical

1 Footballers and dancers usually have a lot of _body_ intelligence.

2 People with _____ intelligence are often good at drawing.

3 My friend, Sally, would like to have more _____ intelligence!

4 Sometimes even young children have good logical- _____ intelligence.

5 If you enjoy being on your own, you probably have a lot of _____ intelligence.

6 You need _____ intelligence to be a good speaker.

7 It's great to go bird-watching with Peter – he's got a lot of _____ intelligence.

8 My brother hasn't got much _____ intelligence.

c **Vocabulary bank** Complete the sentences.

1 My friend telephoned me while I was doing my homework and broke my _concentration_ .

2 Her _____ of European history is amazing.

3 He's got a fantastic _____ and writes brilliant stories.

4 A: Can you give me _____ for the work?
   B: Yes, it will be about £400.

4 Grammar

✱ *must/mustn't* vs. *don't have to*

a Complete the sentences with *must* or *mustn't*.

1 Hurry up, James – we _mustn't_ be late!

2 I _____ remember to phone Sonia tonight.

3 Here's your present. You _____ open it before your birthday!

4 I've told you before – you _____ play football in the street.

5 You _____ forget to lock the door before you leave.

6 If you go to London, you _____ go to the Trocadero – it's great!

7 My old dictionary is useless – I _____ buy a new one.

b Match the sentences with the pictures. Write the correct sentence (*i* or *ii*) for each picture.

1

a   *ii You don't have to eat it.*   b   _____

2

a   _____   b   _____

3

a   _____   b   _____

4

a   _____   b   _____

1   i You mustn't eat it.   ii You don't have to eat it.
2   i She doesn't have to walk.   ii She mustn't walk.
3   i You mustn't look!   ii You don't have to look!
4   i I mustn't move!   ii I don't have to move.

c Circle the correct words.

1   You can borrow it, but you *mustn't* / *don't have to* break it.

2   No, I'm sorry – you *mustn't* / *don't have to* bring your pet into the classroom.

3   It's a secret, OK? You *mustn't* / *don't have to* tell anyone else!

4   Wow! He *mustn't* / *doesn't have to* jump!

5   Stop! You *mustn't* / *don't have to* ride your bikes in the park!

6   I know it's raining, but you *mustn't* / *don't have to* wear all that!

d Complete the sentences with *mustn't* or *don't/doesn't have to*.

1 Be quiet! The baby's asleep, so we _mustn't_ make any noise.

2 My older sister's got a job now, so she _____ ask our parents for pocket money.

3 The homework's easy, so you _____ help me.

4 Don't talk like that, Josh! You _____ be rude to your friends.

5 You _____ borrow my things without asking me!

6 My grandfather's 75, so he _____ pay to travel on the bus.

7 It's a test, so you _____ look at other people's work.

5 Pronunciation

* *mustn't* / (*don't*) *have to*

a ▶ CD3 T25 In the word *mustn't*, the *t* in the middle is not pronounced. Listen and repeat.

1 You mustn't go out.
2 We mustn't be late.
3 You mustn't open it.
4 We mustn't ask questions.

b ▶ CD3 T26 In the phrase *don't have to*, *have to* is pronounced as /hæf tə/. Listen and repeat.

1 I don't have to study hard.
2 You don't have to shout!
3 He doesn't have to go.
4 We don't have to worry.

6 Culture in mind

Answer the questions about Abigail Wilson. Then check with the text on page 72 of the Student's Book.

1 Why wasn't it a surprise when, at the age of 15, Abigail became the youngest black woman ever accepted into university?

   Because she was very talented as a child. _____

2 Why did her parents first think there was something wrong with their daughter?

   _____ .

3 What does the text say about Abigail as a language learner?

   _____ .

4 Does Abigail see herself as a very organised learner?

   _____ .

5 How does she get motivated to study?

   _____ .

6 Why does her mum think it was important for Abigail to learn to play the piano?

   _____ .

7 Study help

* How to study effectively

An important part of learning something is making sure you plan your time and use it well. If you want to remember things well, you need to revise information you've learned. Try to follow this advice:

DO	DON'T
• Make a study timetable at least three weeks before your exams and allow time to relax and have fun. • Revise little and often. • While you're studying, have short regular breaks. A short break every 45 minutes is a good idea. Stand up and walk around – you'll feel more awake! • Try making a week's plan showing what you do every day (school, travel, meals, etc.). You might see where you're wasting time that you could use to study or read.	• Study for hours every night a week before your exams! Studying for hours the night before will make you tired and your brain won't work well. • Study for a long period of time without a break. You probably won't remember information very well if you do this. • Worry too much. If you feel anxious you won't learn as well as if you're relaxed.

Skills in mind

WRITING TIP

Using linkers

Read the short story below. What did the boy in the story think he forgot? _____

> Yesterday I was watching television at home when I _suddenly_ remembered that it was my father's birthday the next day.
>
> I put my coat on quickly, and ¹ _____ I ran outside to catch a bus. I went into a music shop, but I couldn't remember which CD my dad wanted, so I didn't buy anything. ² _____
> I decided to go to the bookshop. I wasn't sure what to get and I stayed there for ages trying to choose a book, but ³ _____ I bought him a book about racing cars.
> ⁴ _____ , I went home again and told my mum about the present. She looked at me strangely for some time, and ⁵ _____ she said, 'But your father's birthday is next month!'

When you are writing a story, you can make it clearer and more interesting by using linking words. Complete the story. Use the linking words in the box.

> then ~~suddenly~~ after that in the end finally then

8 Listen

a ▶ CD3 T27 Jane and Mack are talking together. Jane has had a bad day. Listen to their conversation and write numbers 1–5 in the boxes.

b ▶ CD3 T27 Which of the words in the box in the Writing tip does Jane use in her story? Listen again and tick (✓) the words and phrases you hear.

9 Write

Write a story about when you remembered, or forgot, something very important. Use the questions below and the story in the Writing tip to help you.

- When did your story happen?
- Where were you when you remembered or forgot the important thing? What were you doing?
- What exactly did you forget (or remember)?
- What did you do after that?
- What happened in the end?

Write about 100–120 words.

A

TODAY'S WRITTEN TEST

D

Tony

B

E

C

1

Unit check

1 Fill in the spaces

Complete the text with
the words in the box.

| someone   bad memory   remember   forget   ~~memory~~ |
| remind   memorise   remembers   some of them   imagine |

I think my _memory_ is quite good. I always [1]_____ people's names, and I mean all the
names, not just [2]_____ . When I meet [3]_____ and I hear the person's name,
I [4]_____ that I can see the name written on the person's face. That's how I never
[5]_____ a name. When I have to [6]_____ things for school, I talk aloud while I look at
my notes. My brother says he has a very [7]_____ and he's right! He never [8]_____ his
promises. I always have to [9]_____ him.

9

2 Choose the correct answers

(Circle) the correct answer: a, b or c.

1 _____ said Peter's ill. I think Tom told me.

  a (someone) b no one c everyone

2 He was lying on the ground, but _____ helped
him.

  a no one b everyone c everywhere

3 You _____ tell me again. I'll remember this.

  a don't have to b mustn't c must

4 I think the key is _____ in my room.

  a somewhere b nowhere c everywhere

5 You _____ help me. I can do it myself.

  a must b mustn't c don't have to

6 Joanna _____ buy a new camera. Her old one is
still very good.

  a doesn't have to b mustn't c must

7 You _____ be noisy. Dad is trying to watch TV.

  a must b don't have to c mustn't

8 I wrote letters to ten people, but _____
answered.

  a no one b everyone c something

9 You really _____ forget to lock the door before
you go out.

  a must b mustn't c don't have to

8

3 Vocabulary

Match the two parts of each word or phrase. Then complete the sentences.

re	ral
ac	lures
scatter	minute
seve	~~gular~~
failing	cepted
fai	out
last	at
baby	brained
hangs	talk

1 Abigail's parents read _regular_ bedtime stories to her.

2 Abigail was 15 when she was _____ into university.

3 She says that she doesn't plan and is _____ .

4 _____ _____ playing the piano helped her to see herself as a normal teen.

5 Abigail has studied _____ languages.

6 Her mum thinks that you learn more from your _____ .

7 Abigail says she often delays things up to the _____ _____ .

8 She never did _____ _____ like other babies.

9 Abigail often _____ _____ with friends who are older than her.

8

How did you do?

Total: 25

| ☺ Very good 20 – 25 | 😐 OK 14 – 19 | ☹ Review Unit 9 again 0 – 13 |

Music makers

1 Remember and check

Complete the summary of Carlinhos Brown's story with the words in the box. Then check with the text on page 74 of the Student's Book.

> area   leader   complex
> neighbourhood   albums
> percussionists   tin cans
> violence   pop scene

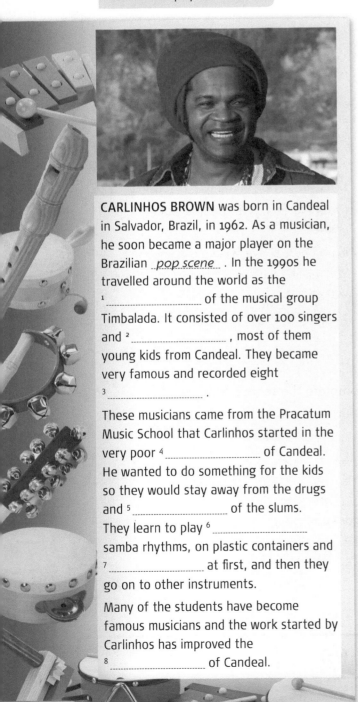

CARLINHOS BROWN was born in Candeal in Salvador, Brazil, in 1962. As a musician, he soon became a major player on the Brazilian _pop scene_ . In the 1990s he travelled around the world as the
¹_____ of the musical group Timbalada. It consisted of over 100 singers and ²_____ , most of them young kids from Candeal. They became very famous and recorded eight
³_____ .

These musicians came from the Pracatum Music School that Carlinhos started in the very poor ⁴_____ of Candeal. He wanted to do something for the kids so they would stay away from the drugs and ⁵_____ of the slums. They learn to play ⁶_____ samba rhythms, on plastic containers and
⁷_____ at first, and then they go on to other instruments.

Many of the students have become famous musicians and the work started by Carlinhos has improved the
⁸_____ of Candeal.

2 Grammar

* Present perfect continuous

a Match the pictures with the sentences. Write numbers 1–6 in the boxes.

1   You've been sitting there for 20 minutes. What's wrong with you?

2   Where's my mobile phone? I've been looking for it all morning!

3   Let's stop and have a drink. We've been playing for two hours!

4   I've been trying really hard to understand this. But my French isn't good enough.

5   He's been crying since nine o'clock. What can we do?

6   We've been sitting here all morning. Let's go for a walk.

b Complete the dialogues. Use the present perfect continuous form of the verbs in brackets.

1   Cathy: I'm surprised that Paul speaks Spanish.

   Claire: Why? He _'s been learning_ (learn) it for years.

2   Nick: _____ you _____ (try) to phone me?

   Joanna: Yes, all morning.

3   James: There are terrible floods in the south!

   Annie: I'm not surprised. It _____ (rain) for ten days.

4   Sam: I _____ (tidy up) since eight thirty!

   Sue: I can help you if you want.

5   Marek: Look. Harry's got a digital camera.

   Piotr: So what? I _____ (use) a digital camera since 2003.

6   Penny: Luisa looks really tired! What _____ (do)?

   Mark: I think she _____ (run).

c Use the words to write sentences. Use the present perfect continuous.

1 Phil / live / in London / for ten years
  Phil has been living in London for ten years.

2 I / work / really hard
  _____ .

3 The sun / shine / all day
  _____ .

4 She / not study / hard enough
  _____ .

5 You / eat / all morning
  _____ .

6 you / wait / long
  _____ ?

7 he / clean / his car
  _____ ?

③ Grammar

✱ Present perfect continuous and present perfect simple

a Match the pictures with the sentences. Write numbers 1–6 in the boxes.

1 Well, I haven't been feeling well for a week.
2 I've been going to the gym three times a week for a year.
3 No, I've been sitting here for half an hour.
4 Yes, I do, but I've forgotten your name. Sorry.
5 Thanks. My father's been teaching me since I was three.
6 I know. Five people have already told me.

(A) 4
Don't you remember me?

(B)
COUGH!
What's wrong with you?

(C)
Your T-shirt's dirty.

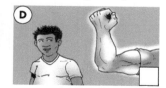
(D)
You're really fit!

(E)
You're really good!

(F)
Have you just got home?

b Tick (✓) the correct sentence in each pair. Put a cross (✗) next to the incorrect sentence.

1 a Maria has had her car for 11 years. ✓
  b Maria has been having her car for 11 years. ✗

2 a I've been meeting your sister three or four times. ☐
  b I've met your sister three or four times. ☐

3 a Jack's playing football. He has scored two goals. ☐
  b Jack's playing football. He has been scoring two goals. ☐

4 a They've been buying a new house and they really like it. ☐
  b They've bought a new house and they really like it. ☐

5 a I've been reading this book for nine days, but I still haven't finished it! ☐
  b I've read this book for nine days, but I still haven't finished it! ☐

6 a Ouch! I've been burning my finger! ☐
  b Ouch! I've burned my finger! ☐

c Complete the sentences. Use the present perfect simple or present perfect continuous form of the verbs in brackets.

1 I *'ve met* (meet) three friends this morning.

2 My brother _____ always _____ (want) to meet your sister.

3 I hope my teacher won't be angry. I _____ (forget) my homework.

4 Great! I _____ (do) all my homework. Now I can watch TV.

5 She's awful. She _____ (talk) about herself all evening.

6 He _____ (write) four emails this morning.

7 My father _____ (use) the computer since eight o'clock this morning!

8 We _____ (tidy) our bedroom all morning.

d Read the information about film star, Arnold Schwarzenegger. Then complete the dialogue.

A: Where is he from?

B: He was born in ___Austria___ and he lived there for about [1] _____ years.

A: How long [2] _____ (live) in the USA?

B: For more than [3] _____ years.

A: How many films [4] _____ (make)?

B: More than [5] _____ .

A: How long [6] _____ (be married)?

B: Since 1986.

A: How long [7] _____ (work) with the Special Olympics?

B: For more than 25 years.

ARNOLD SCHWARZENEGGER

born 1947 near Graz in Austria

moved to the USA in 1968

married Maria Shriver in 1986

more than 30 films, including:
The Terminator, Eraser, True Lies

work with the Special Olympics since 1978

4 Pronunciation

❋ Sentence stress: rhythm

▶ CD3 T28 Underline the words you think are stressed. Then listen, check and repeat.

1 A: How <u>long</u> have you been <u>waiting</u>?

   B: I've been waiting for three hours!

2 A: Where's she been living?

   B: She's been living in London.

3 A: What's he been doing?

   B: He's been looking for a new flat.

5 Vocabulary

❋ Music and musical instruments

a Put the letters in the correct order. Then complete the sentences.

1 _Country_ music is very popular in the Southern and Western USA. (rcoynut)

2 Mick Jagger is a famous _____ singer. (orkc)

3 _____ is very popular amongst teens these days. (pih-poh)

4 Yo-Yo Ma plays _____ music. (aascsicll)

5 Which do you prefer, _____ or _____ ? (zajz / gareag)

b Fill in the crossword.

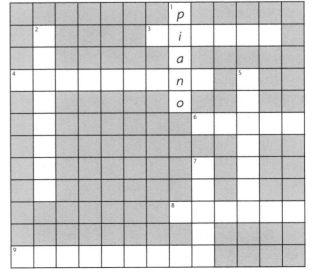

								p					
	2				3			i					
								a					
4								n			5		
								o					
									6				
									7				
							8						
9													

c (Circle) the correct words.

1 I love the first song on the latest Duffy
(album) / single.

2 Oh, no! I left my *stereo / MP3* on the bus
this morning.

3 I love listening to *live / recorded* music.
It's great to see the bands.

4 My parents are buying a new *stereo /
personal stereo* for our living room.

5 I never buy *albums / singles*. I think
they're too expensive for just one song.

d **Vocabulary bank** Write the words for
the definitions.

1 the words of a song _lyrics_

2 a large group of musicians
_____

3 the person who directs the performance
of musicians _____

4 the place where recordings are made
_____

5 a group of singers _____

6 a concert that takes place in a park or a
stadium _____

---

7 **Study help**

✱ Vocabulary: knowing a word

When you record vocabulary in your
notebook, it's important to record more than
just the meaning of the word. It might also
be a good idea to record these things:

a the pronunciation and where the main stress is

b what part of speech the new word is (a noun,
verb, etc.)

c other words that go together with the new
word (For example, if it is a noun, what verbs
go with it?)

d an example sentence with the new word
(You'll need to know how to use it!)

e the spelling (Be careful when you record
the word to write it correctly!)

Look at examples 1–5. Match them with one
of the tips a–e above.

1 an effort: to make an effort	c
2 live music (adj.)	
3 ~~keybaords~~ keyboards	
4 enough: /ɪˈnʌf/	
5 musical instrument: I'd like to learn how to play a musical instrument.	

---

6 **Everyday English**

Complete the dialogues. Use the expressions in the box.

| I'm just saying that | Check it out | ~~I have to say~~ | got nothing to do with | What do you mean | loads of |

1 A: Do you like my tattoo?

B: Erm, well, no, not very much. _I have to say_ I don't really like tattoos.

2 A: I'm hungry. Let's get a pizza.

B: OK. We can go to the shopping centre – there are _____ good places there.

3 A: Have you heard any good music recently?

B: Yes, I have. There's this new CD by Kaiser Chiefs. _____ – I think you'll like it!

4 A: Don't go to that café. 'The Bakehouse' is nicer.

B: Oh? Is that café really bad, then?

A: No – _____ there are better places to go.

5 A: I'm surprised that you're wearing a yellow dress.

B: _____ ?

A: Just that you look better in other colours!

6 A: Oh, are you reading a letter? Who wrote it? Your boyfriend?

B: Oh Pauline, go away! It's _____ you, OK?

Skills in mind

READING TIP

Matching descriptions

In some tests and examinations (for example in PET), you have to read a text and match things. Do this:

- First, read the descriptions of the people carefully because there are clues about the kinds of things they like. Read the description of Carol Morgan in Exercise 8. From this description we know that she really likes jazz music, and that she doesn't like piano music.

- Next, read the book, film or music descriptions. Remember: you don't need to understand every word – just look for ideas that go together with the people. Read the descriptions in Exercise 8 quickly. We know that Carol Morgan likes jazz music. Which two CDs are jazz? Read those descriptions again. We know Carol doesn't like piano music, so which CD is best for her?

- There will usually be more books, films or music than people – so be careful!

8 Read

The people below all want to buy a CD. Read the descriptions of six CDs and decide which one is right for each person. Write the number of the CD in the boxes.

a Carol Morgan likes many kinds of music, but her favourite is jazz. The only music she really doesn't like is piano music, even if it's jazz. `6`

b Mark Moloney doesn't care very much about music, but he likes to have soft, gentle music playing in his flat sometimes. He isn't keen on classical or jazz music, but he likes piano playing. ☐

c Andrea Bolton likes all kinds of music, but her favourite instrument is the electric guitar – she's a big fan of Eric Clapton, for example. She also likes folk music. ☐

d Dave Stone only likes instrumental music – he never buys anything vocal. He likes rock and pop, but his preference is for classical music. ☐

This week's NEW MUSIC RELEASES

1 The Best of Keith Jarrett
The maestro of jazz piano continues to astound audiences around the world. This collection of his greatest work includes The Köln Concert, Part 1 and extracts from the Paris Concert as well. Excellent value and a must for all jazz lovers. £12.99

2 Richard Thompson 1985–2005
Thompson's stunning electric guitar playing, and his folk-rock songs, are gathered together on a 2-CD collection that shows the best of his work over the last two decades. £18.99

3 Richard Clayderman
French pianist, known for his relaxing piano music, has this new collection out on CD. Ideal as a present for the person who likes relaxing background music. £9.99

4 The Monteverdi Vespers of 1610
This new recording of Monteverdi's great choral work is excellent, with great singing from the Milton Keynes Chorus. Classical music lovers will want to add this one to their collections. £24.99 for the 2-CD set

5 The Best of Paco Peña
The great classical guitarist shows all his brilliance in this new collection. Works by Vila-Lobos and Haydn, amongst others. Great value at only £9.99

6 Wynton Marsalis
The great jazz trumpeter has put together some of his best-known numbers and a few new pieces on this magical set. Perhaps not as classy as his last offering, but all jazz aficionados will want this one anyway. £13.99

9 Write

Write a text about a CD that you have bought recently and really like. Say:

- who the CD is by and what it is called
- why you decided to buy it
- what kind of music is on the CD
- which songs/tracks are your special favourites and why
- how it compares to other CDs in your collection

Unit check

1 Fill in the spaces

Complete the text with the words in the box.

| singer   drums   saxophone   listen   ~~classical~~   plays |
| have been playing   has been collecting   has collected   jazz |

My father loves _classical_ music – he ¹_____ records of Mozart's music for 15 years, and I think he ²_____ over 300 records so far! My mother was a ³_____ when she was younger, but now she prefers to ⁴_____ to music. My cousins, Jim and Sandra, ⁵_____ in a band for three years. Sandra ⁶_____ the guitar (she's really good) and Jim sings. What about me? Well, two years ago my parents bought me some ⁷_____ , and now I am in a ⁸_____ band with three friends from school. My friend, Angus, is a great ⁹_____ player!

9

2 Choose the correct answers

(Circle) the correct answer: a, b or c.

1 I'm tired. I _____ for ten hours.

  a (ve been working)   b 've worked   c work

2 They're angry. They _____ for ages.

  a are waiting   b waited   c 've been waiting

3 Tina _____ six books by John Grisham.

  a has been reading   b have read   c has read

4 How long _____ ? The park is flooded!

  a is it raining   b has it been raining

  c was it raining

5 David _____ in a band since 2001.

  a is playing   b has been playing   c plays

6 Look! Someone _____ that window.

  a have broken   b has broken

  c has been breaking

7 We _____ Karen for years.

  a 've been knowing   b know   c 've known

8 There's a new film at the cinema – _____ it?

  a do you see   b have you been seeing

  c have you seen

9 She _____ on the phone for an hour!

  a 's talked   b 's been talking   c talk

8

3 Vocabulary

Write the words under the pictures.

1 _drums_

2 _____

3 _____

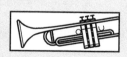
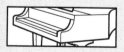

4 _____

5 _____

6 _____

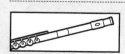
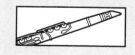
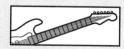

7 _____

8 _____

9 _____

8

How did you do?

Total: **25**

|  Very good 20 – 25 | OK 14 – 19 | 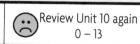 Review Unit 10 again 0 – 13 |

11 A visit to the doctor's

1 Vocabulary

* Medicine

a Complete the sentences with the words in the box.

> health   epidemic   hospital   ~~ambulance~~   hurts   injection
> painful   patients   tablet   treat   antiseptic

1   There was an accident in town yesterday – I saw
    the __ambulance__ arriving.

2   My sister's a nurse – she works in the
    _____ in town.

3   When the dentist took my tooth out, it was quite
    _____ .

4   You shouldn't smoke – it's bad for your
    _____ .

5   I went to the doctor yesterday. I had to wait
    a long time because there were lots of other
    _____ .

6   Before the doctor gives you the
    _____ , she'll clean your skin
    with some _____ .

7   If you've got a headache, take a
    _____ – an aspirin, for example.

8   I had a bad stomach ache, so I took some
    medicine to _____ it.

9   I fell over when I was playing football, and
    now my ankle really _____ !

10 Hundreds of people got ill – it was a flu
    _____ .

b **Vocabulary bank** Match the sentences.

1   Why has James got a bandage round his hand?
2   Have you taken your temperature?
3   Why is your aunt in a wheelchair?
4   Why doesn't your sister eat yoghurt?
5   Is Jane coming to the meeting?
6   How are you doing with your leg in plaster?

a   Yes, it's 36.5° – everything's perfectly normal.
b   She's allergic to dairy products.
c   No, she can't. She's gone down with flu.
d   He cut himself when he broke a window.
e   Well, it's not easy to be on crutches!
f   She fell from a tree years ago. She can't walk.

c Complete the sentences with the words in the box.

> hurt   pain   sore   surgeon   stomach ache   temperature   ~~toothache~~   vaccination

1   I've got __toothache__ .

2   Oh, that's better! My feet really _____ .

3   Jack feels ill, so his mum's taking his _____ .

4   I ate too much at lunchtime and now I've got
    _____ .

5   I've got a bad cold and a very _____ throat.

6   I've got a _____ in my arm.

7   Don't worry about the operation – the
    _____ is one of the best in the country.

8   At school they gave us all a _____ to stop us
    getting flu this winter.

2 Grammar

✻ Defining relative clauses

a (Circle) the correct words.

1 My mother loves London – it's the city (*where*) / *that* she was born.

2 There's Jim – he's the boy *which* / *who* had a party last weekend.

3 Last night there was a dog *which* / *who* was making a lot of noise.

4 The shopping centre is the place *who* / *where* I meet my friends at the weekend.

5 Don't go to that dentist! He's the one *where* / *who* never smiles!

6 I prefer the teachers *which* / *who* don't give us too much homework!

7 That's the shop *where* / *which* I bought my new DVD player.

b Complete the sentences with *which, that, where* or *who*. Sometimes there is more than one correct answer.

1 Alberto Santos Dumont was a Brazilian *who* designed planes and balloons.

2 In 1897 he went to Paris, the city _____ he made his first flight in a balloon.

3 In 1909, he built a small plane _____ was called 'The Grasshopper'.

4 There is now an airport in Rio de Janeiro _____ is named after him.

5 Martin Luther King was a man _____ tried to make life better for African-Americans in the USA.

6 In 1963, he made a speech _____ became very famous – the 'I have a dream' speech.

7 Memphis is the city _____ King was killed in 1968.

8 The man _____ shot Martin Luther King was James Earl Ray.

c Match the two parts of the sentences. Then write them with a correct relative pronoun.

1 Usain Bolt was the man
2 Andalusia is a place in Spain
3 Lyon is a city in France
4 Evaporation is a process
5 'Crocodile nests' are huts
6 Pompeii is the city

a you can spend a holiday in a cave.
b puts water back into the atmosphere.
c started a free bicycle scheme many years ago.
d was destroyed in the year 79 AD.
e set a new world record for the 100 metres at the Beijing Olympics.
f are used in a ceremony in Papua New Guinea.

1 *Usain Bolt was the man who set a new world record for the 100 metres at the Beijing Olympics.*

2 _____ .

3 _____ .

4 _____ .

5 _____ .

6 _____ .

3 Grammar

✻ used to

a Put the words in order to make the sentences or questions.

1 used / I / play / a / to / football / of / lot
   I used to play a lot of football.

2 go / used / we / to / park / the / to
   _____ .

3 shop / cheap / that / be / used / very / to
   _____ .

4 father / to / your / the guitar / play / a / band / use / in / did
   _____ ?

5 Maths / didn't / to / brother / enjoy / use / my
   _____ .

b Complete the sentences. Use the correct form of the verb in brackets in the present simple or *used to*.

1 I _didn't use to have_ (not have) a mobile phone, but now I _send_ (send) text messages every day.

2 I _____ (like) chips, but now I _____ (eat) fruit and salad.

3 We _____ (play) tennis every day, but now we _____ (not play) it any more.

4 There _____ (be) three cinemas in our town, but now there _____ (be) only one.

5 We _____ (not go) on holiday when I was young, but now we _____ (go) to Spain every year.

6 My sister _____ (love) rock music, but she _____ (hate) it when she was younger.

7 I _____ (not read) books when I was a child, but now I _____ (read) four every week!

8 A: _____ you _____ (go) to bed early when you were a child?

    B: Yes, I did, but now I _____ (stay) up as late as I want!

c Look at the pairs of pictures and write a sentence for each pair.

How Anna has changed!

Before   After

1 Anna used to *eat chips, but now she eats salad.*

Before   After

2 She used to go _____ .

Before   After

3 She _____ .

Before   After

4 _____ .

Before   After

5 _____ .

Before   After

6 _____ .

d Write true sentences about you and your friends or family. Use *used to* or *didn't use to* and the ideas in the box.

music   sports   food   TV   school   home   family

I used to play the piano, but now I play the guitar. My sister ... _____

_____

_____

4 Pronunciation

a ▶ **CD3 T29** Listen to the verb *use* in these sentences. (Circle) it when it has a /s/ sound. Underline it when it has a /z/ sound.

1 We <u>used</u> the Internet to find the information.
2 I used to go to bed early when I was young.
3 Who used my personal stereo?
4 My dad used to work in an office.
5 Did he use to play tennis?
6 Did she use my bike?

b ▶ **CD3 T29** Do you hear the *d* in the word *used*? Listen, check and repeat.

5 Culture in mind

Put the lines in order to make a summary of the text 'Doctors without Borders'.
Then check with the text on page 86 of the Student's Book.

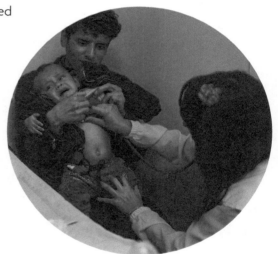

	almost 60 different countries. The organisation has helped
	and women who work for the organisation.
	victims in disaster situations in many countries
	kidnapped or killed. In 1999, MSF won the Nobel
1	Médecins Sans Frontières is a non-political
	all over the world – in earthquakes, famines or wars.
	organisation with its headquarters in Geneva,
	Peace Prize. The prize honours the courage of the men
	Switzerland. It has about 3,000 volunteer doctors in
	volunteers. They are sometimes attacked,
	Work for MSF is often very dangerous for the

6 Study help

✳ Using the internet

The internet is a great way for you to practise and use your English! Here are some ideas:

- Visit websites for people who are learning English, with exercises for grammar and vocabulary, and interesting reading and listening texts. Try, for example, the *English in Mind* website: www.cambridge.org/elt/englishinmind. The BBC website is also excellent: www.bbc.co.uk/worldservice/learningenglish.

- Find websites in English that have information about things you're interested in: for example, sports, cinema, music, etc. Use: www.google.com or www.yahoo.com to find good pages in English.

- You can usually copy articles and save them on your computer. Sometimes there are also interviews you can listen to, if you want to practise your listening skills. You can also download podcasts from the radio.

- Be careful! Many websites from non-English-speaking countries have versions in English. Sometimes it's good English, but not always! It's often safer if you go to websites from the UK (addresses end in *.uk*), Australia (addresses end in *.au*) or the United States (addresses end in *.com*, *.org* or *.ac*).

Skills in mind

7 Listen

▶ **CD3 T30** Listen to six short recordings and (circle) the correct answers.

1 Where are these people?
   a at a bus stop   b (in an airport)   c in a restaurant

2 Who are the people talking?
   a strangers   b child and parent   c friends at school

3 Where are these people?
   a in a shop   b on a train   c in a library

4 Who are the people talking?
   a strangers   b child and parent   c friends at school

5 Where are these people?
   a in a plane   b in a restaurant   c in a car

6 Who are the people talking?
   a teacher and student
   b mother and daughter   c friends at school

LISTENING TIP

Identifying places and speakers

When you listen to recordings you often need to identify where, or who, the people are. In some examinations you listen to a recording and choose from three or four possible answers.

- Always listen to the whole recording. **Never** choose your answer before the recording has finished.

- Look at **Exercise 7 question 1**, for example. You'll hear someone say that she missed the bus so you might think it's a bus stop. But be careful! The other person later says 'The plane's delayed', and finally, he says 'before we **check in** for our **flight**', so what's the correct answer?

8 Read

a Who is the man in the photo? Why do you think he is famous? Read the text quickly to find the answers.

Christiaan Barnard

These days, people with severe heart problems can have a heart transplant – in other words, another heart is put into their body to replace the heart with problems.

Christiaan Barnard was the surgeon who performed the first human heart-transplant operation. Barnard was born in 1922, in his native South Africa. He studied medicine at the University of Cape Town and graduated in 1953. Then he went to the USA and studied at the University of Minnesota. He returned to the University of Cape Town in 1958 to teach surgery. No one knew very much about him – but in 1967, he became world-famous.

On 3 December, Barnard transferred the heart of a 25-year-old woman into the body of Louis Washkansky, a 55-year-old grocer. Unfortunately, Washkansky died 18 days later. Barnard did a second transplant, on 2 January 1968, for a man called Philip Blaiberg – this was a lot more successful, as

Blaiberg lived for just over 18 months after the operation.

Barnard was not the usual picture of a surgeon. Young and handsome, he spent as much time in nightclubs as he did in operating theatres. He met the Pope in Rome and President Lyndon Johnson in the USA. He knew many beautiful film stars of the time, like Sophia Loren, but all three of his marriages failed. He also performed free surgery on hundreds of very sick people.

He died in September 2001, aged 78.

b Read the text again and answer the questions.

1 What nationality was Christiaan Barnard?

   He was South African.

2 In which two countries did he study?

   ----

3 When did he become famous?

   ----

4 Who was the first person to get a heart transplant?

   ----

5 How long did Philip Blaiberg live after his heart transplant?

   ----

6 In what ways was Barnard different from other surgeons?

Unit check

1 Fill in the spaces

Complete the text with the words in the box.

> hurts   who   sore throat   treat   ended up with
> temperature   ~~health problems~~   pain   ambulance   that

I never usually have __health problems__ but two days ago I had to study for my maths test. After five hours I
¹_____ toothache! My dad took me to see a dentist, ²_____ said the real problem was
a 'complete unwillingness to study'. Anyway, I didn't do the test, so I have to do it tomorrow. Right now I'm
in bed. I'm really hot – I think I've got a ³_____ of about 40°, and I have a really bad ⁴_____ ,
so I can hardly talk. A minute ago I wanted to take a tablet to stop the ⁵_____ , so I got out of bed
and fell over some maths books ⁶_____ were on the floor. Now I can't stand up because my ankle
⁷_____ ! I think Dad should call an ⁸_____ to take me to hospital. I'm sure the doctors there
will know how to ⁹_____ me!

9

2 Choose the correct answers

(Circle) the correct answer: a, b or c.

1 I'd like to live in a place _____ the sun shines all the time.
   a which   b that   c (where)

2 Your doctor can give you a tablet _____ will stop the pain.
   a where   b who   c that

3 Who's the man _____ made this film?
   a that   b which   c where

4 The jeans _____ were in the window were really expensive.
   a where   b who   c that

5 The people _____ saw the match were lucky.
   a where   b which   c that

6 Those are the boys _____ broke our window.
   a who   b which   c where

7 Did you _____ to like going to the dentist?
   a used   b use   c not

8 In the past, people _____ illnesses with strange methods.
   a used   b used to treat   c use to treat

9 We _____ enjoy running, but now we love it!
   a usedn't to   b didn't use to   c used to not

8

3 Vocabulary

Put the letters in the correct order. Then complete the sentences.

1 The __ambulance__ arrived only a few minutes after the accident. (ualanbcme)

2 The disease affected so many people that it was a real _____ . (pcmeeidi)

3 To make sure you don't get flu again, why don't you have a _____ ? (vinctiacaon)

4 Claire had a bad accident and the _____ had to operate on her for hours. (rgusone)

5 My aunt is a doctor and her _____ like her a lot. (eatnpits)

6 A: Look, I've cut my finger. B: You should put some _____ on it. (tptiaicsen)

7 I didn't feel better after three weeks, so the doctor had to give me an _____ . (oennjctii)

8 I drank a lot of cold fruit juice and got a bad _____ ache. (chastmo)

9 My dad was treated for heart problems because he had a pain in his _____ . (stehc)   8

How did you do?

Total: 25

| 😊 | Very good 20 – 25 | 😐 | OK 14 – 19 | 😞 | Review Unit 11 again 0 – 13 |

12 If I had ...

1 Remember and check

There is one mistake in each sentence. <u>Underline</u> it and write the correct answer.
Then check with the text on page 88 of the Student's Book.

1 Kylie has her own <u>web page</u> on myspace.com. _blog_

2 Brett frequently posts blogs. ....

3 Kylie hates a website called agirlsworld.com. ....

4 Kylie sometimes sends her own designs to podcasts. ....

5 Brett prefers videocasts to websites. ....

6 Brett would love to work as a computer programmer. ....

2 Grammar

✱ Second conditional

a Match the pictures with the sentences. Write 1–6 in the boxes.

1 If I was taller, I'd get it and eat it.

2 If I had enough money, I'd live in a hot, dry country.

3 If I had a bicycle, I wouldn't walk to school any more.

4 If we didn't have so much homework, we'd go to the beach.

5 I'd stop them if I was bigger.

6 We'd win more games if we were taller.

b (Circle) the correct words.

1 If we (had) / would have a bigger house, I had / ('d have) my own bedroom.

2 If I had / 'd have more money, I went / 'd go and visit my uncle in America.

3 If we didn't / wouldn't have a dog, our house smelled / would smell better.

4 I liked / 'd like our town more if there were / would be more places for teenagers.

5 I bought / 'd buy a DVD player if they weren't / wouldn't be so expensive.

6 We went / 'd go out if we didn't / wouldn't have so much homework.

c Complete the sentences. Use the correct form of the verbs in brackets.

1 If I ___was___ (be) older, I _'d leave_ (leave) school.

2 If my brother .... (leave) home, I .... (have) his bedroom.

3 If I .... (know) the answers, I .... (tell) you!

4 Your parents .... (be) angry if they .... (know) what you've done.

5 If we .... (not have) a TV, ... you .... (read) more books?

6 If you .... (not eat) so much chocolate, you .... (not be) overweight.

d Rewrite the sentences using the second conditional.

1 I don't have a bicycle, so I walk to school.
   If I had a bicycle, I wouldn't walk to school.

2 We haven't got a computer, so we don't send emails.
   ....

3 I love music, so I spend all my money on CDs.
   ....

4 I'm not a good player, so I'm not in the school team.
   ....

5 I do a lot of exercise, so I'm very fit.
   ....

6 My uncle speaks good English, so he watches American TV programmes.
   ....

e Write true sentences about you or people you know. Use your own ideas or the ideas in the box.

school
money
sports
travel
computers
friends and family

If I didn't have so much homework, I'd go out every night.
....
....
....
....

f Match the problems with the possible advice.

1 I've got a terrible headache!
2 I'm bored!
3 I'm really cold in here!
4 I find the grammar very hard!
5 I need information for my project!
6 My eyesight's bad. I can't read the board!

a If I were you, I'd close the window.
b I'd talk to the teacher if I were you.
c If I were you, I'd get some glasses.
d If I were you, I'd take an aspirin.
e I'd play a computer game if I were you.
f If I were you, I'd search the internet.

g Write some advice for the people in the pictures. Use the second conditional.

1 *If I were you, I'd go to the dentist.*

2 ....

3 ....

4 ....

5 ....

6 ....

① I've got toothache!

② I'm so tired!

③ I'm really, really hungry!

④ I've got a big problem at school!

⑤ I can't sleep!

⑥ I don't understand this!

ENGLISH GAMMAR

③ Vocabulary

⭐ Information technology and computers

a Complete the text with the words in the box.

> run ~~logged on~~ touch pad surf printer password USB stick
> download keyboard hard disk crashed saved screen

It was so strange the other day. I had just _logged on_ to my laptop to ¹_____ the web for a while when I suddenly heard this noise. I could also see some colour changes on the ²_____ , so I got a bit worried. I checked the ³_____ – it was OK, I could type without any problems. I switched on the ⁴_____ – it worked all right, in colour and in black and white. I checked the mouse and the ⁵_____ – everything was OK. Then I rang up a friend. She suggested I should ⁶_____ a virus checker programme. I managed to ⁷_____ one for free. When I wanted to key in the ⁸_____ , a message said 'There's a problem with your ⁹_____ .' I panicked and ¹⁰_____ my most important files on a ¹¹_____ .

Then my laptop shut down. The hard disk ¹²_____ ! Now I don't know if I should call myself lucky or unlucky!

b Complete the words.

1 I spend quite some time online in c _h_ _a_ t r o _o_ _m_ _s_ .

2 I need to get an a __ __ p __ __ r because I'm going to take my laptop to Britain.

3 When you look for something on the web, which __ e __ r __ h __ n __ __ ne do you use?

4 There was a problem with my internet connection last night and I was __ __ f __ i n __ for hours.

5 Some new laptops don't have any CD __ __ i __ es any more.

6 I can't switch on my computer. There's a problem with the p __ w __ __ __ e a __ .

c Vocabulary bank Look at the pictures and fill in the word puzzle.

What's the mystery word? _____

4 Pronunciation

*'d

a ▶ CD3 T31 Listen and (circle) the words you hear.

1 *I open / (I'd open)* the window.

2 *They eat / They'd eat* meat.

3 *I ask / I'd ask* the teacher lots of questions.

4 *We love / We'd love* tuna sandwiches for lunch.

5 *They listen / They'd listen* to music.

6 *We have / We'd have* a really good time.

b ▶ CD3 T31 Listen again and repeat the sentences.

5 Everyday English

a Complete the expressions. Use the words in the box.

good ~~like~~ same shame show worth

1 Looks ___like___

2 It's a _____

3 It's no _____

4 at the _____ time

5 It's not _____ it

6 It just goes to _____

b Complete the dialogues. Use the expressions from Exercise 5a.

1 A: Hey – try one of these new biscuits. They're delicious, and *at the same time* , they're good for you!

B: OK. Let me try one. Ugh – it's horrible.

A: But it's good for you!

B: [1] _____ – I can't eat it.

A: Well, [2] _____ – some people don't understand good food!

2 A: Hey look. The Lamas are playing a concert here next month! But look at the price.

B: Yeah. They're a really good band, but eighty pounds? [3] _____ .

A: [4] _____ we aren't going to the concert.

B: That's right. [5] _____ , though. I like them a lot.

6 Study help

* How to give a good presentation

You may have to give a presentation in English at school, for an examination, or in your future job. Here are some tips:

- Find the information you need for your talk well before the day of the presentation. You can find lots of information in libraries or on the internet.

- Make notes. Write down the most important words. You don't need to write sentences because it isn't usually a good idea to read aloud. A good speaker will look at the audience, not at his or her piece of paper.

- Make sure your presentation has a good, interesting start and ending. They are what your audience will remember most.

- Find pictures, diagrams, graphs, etc. to show your audience if you can. This always helps listeners to enjoy a talk and listen carefully.

- Some time before your presentation – ideally the day before – practise what you are going to say. You can do this alone, of course. If there is a time limit, time yourself to make sure your talk isn't too long or too short.

- Before you begin your talk, try not to feel nervous. It's a good idea to try relaxation exercises, for example deep breathing, and positive thinking!

Skills in mind

7 Read

Read the text and (circle) the correct answer: a, b, c or d.

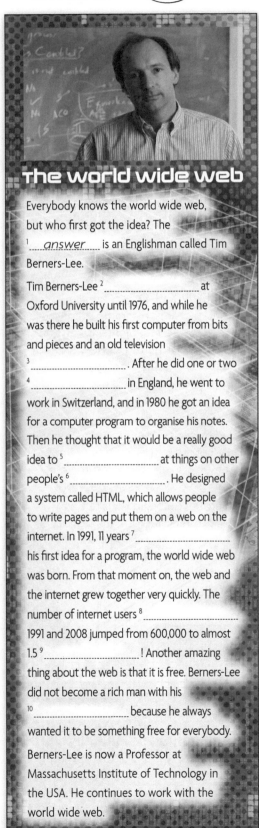

the world wide web

Everybody knows the world wide web, but who first got the idea? The
[1] _____answer_____ is an Englishman called Tim Berners-Lee.

Tim Berners-Lee [2] _____ at Oxford University until 1976, and while he was there he built his first computer from bits and pieces and an old television [3] _____. After he did one or two [4] _____ in England, he went to work in Switzerland, and in 1980 he got an idea for a computer program to organise his notes. Then he thought that it would be a really good idea to [5] _____ at things on other people's [6] _____. He designed a system called HTML, which allows people to write pages and put them on a web on the internet. In 1991, 11 years [7] _____ his first idea for a program, the world wide web was born. From that moment on, the web and the internet grew together very quickly. The number of internet users [8] _____ 1991 and 2008 jumped from 600,000 to almost 1.5 [9] _____! Another amazing thing about the web is that it is free. Berners-Lee did not become a rich man with his [10] _____ because he always wanted it to be something free for everybody.

Berners-Lee is now a Professor at Massachusetts Institute of Technology in the USA. He continues to work with the world wide web.

	a	b	c	d
1	idea	answer	name	question
2	studied	went	wanted	did
3	film	set	programme	channel
4	televisions	jobs	works	companies
5	look	see	read	listen
6	books	webs	computers	televisions
7	before	when	after	until
8	as	to	from	between
9	billion	thousand	users	more
10	money	discovery	internet	invention

READING TIP

Multiple choice cloze texts

In many examinations (for example, PET) you read a gapped text and choose words that fill the spaces. It tests your vocabulary and grammar. Remember:

- Read the complete text first, before you answer the questions. You can't do the exercise well if you don't understand the whole text, and sometimes the information you need is after the space.

- Read all the possible answers carefully. Sometimes one or more answers are clearly wrong. Identify them first and put a line through them. Look at **Exercise 7**. In number 1, *d* (*question*) is clearly wrong, so put a line through it.

- Read the words before and after the gap before you choose your answer. For example, in **Exercise 7**, the sentence before space number 1 is a question, so the correct answer is *b* (*answer*). In number 2, *b* (*went*) is not the correct answer, because the word after the space is *at*, and people say *went/go to*, not *went ~~at~~*.

8 Write

Write a paragraph about how the internet has changed people's lives since 1991. Use these questions:

- What do you and people you know use the internet for?

- How do you think people did these things before 1991?

- Do you think there are things you can do on the internet that people couldn't do at all in the past?

- Do you think the internet and web have improved people's lives? Why / Why not?

Unit check

1 Fill in the spaces

Complete the text with the words in the box.

crashes   didn't   downloads   Net   screen   had   logs on   ~~computer~~   printer   search

My father is a journalist and he uses an old __computer__ to write. He doesn't take a ¹_____ with him when he travels. He just looks at the text on the ²_____ , corrects it and then ³_____ to the internet and sends the text to his newspaper. He also uses the ⁴_____ when he wants to ⁵_____ for information. When he ⁶_____ files, he always burns a CD so that he has copies – his computer isn't very good and often ⁷_____ . He says that if he ⁸_____ enough money, he'd buy a better computer. My mother says that he'd have more money if he ⁹_____ spend it so quickly!

9

2 Choose the correct answers

(Circle) the correct answer: a, b or c.

1   Claire would find a lot of information if she _____ on the internet.

   a looks   **b** would look   **c** (looked)

2   I wouldn't do that if I _____ you.

   a am   **b** would be   **c** were

3   If I _____ more about it, I'd help you.

   a would know   **b** knew   **c** know

4   We're going to launch our own _____ .

   a computer   **b** internet   **c** website

5   David would like that joke if he _____ here.

   a was   **b** would be   **c** is

6   If you _____ any film, which one would it be?

   a can watch   **b** could watch   **c** watched

7   What _____ they do if we went to the police?

   a would   **b** will   **c** were

8   My friend sometimes spends hours _____ the internet.

   a looking   **b** surfing   **c** watching

9   If Mary found that book, she _____ it.

   a 'd buy   **b** bought   **c** 'll buy

8

3 Vocabulary

Match the two parts of each word or phrase. Then complete the sentences.

USB	engine	1 I normally use a mouse. I don't like using the _touch pad_ .
search	~~pad~~	2 How many _____ _____ does your new laptop have?
~~touch~~	lead	3 I think Google is the most frequently used _____ _____ .
pro	vider	4 Can you put those files on a _____ _____ for me?
power	tor	5 I can't switch the laptop on. The _____ _____ seems to be broken.
USB	ser	6 Are you happy with your internet _____ ? Mine doesn't offer a very good service.
brow	board	7 I need an _____ so I can plug my laptop in here.
key	slots	8 Peter's got a problem with his _____ . The 'R' key doesn't work properly.
adap	stick	9 I'm using a new internet _____ , and it's much faster than my old one was.

8

How did you do?

Total: **25**

:)	Very good 20 – 25	:|	OK 14 – 19	:(	Review Unit 12 again 0 – 13

Lost worlds

1 Grammar

✱ Past perfect

a Read the story, and then number the pictures to show the order in which the events happened. Write numbers 1–8 in the boxes.

> When Mrs Johnson got home last Wednesday, she found a terrible mess in her living room. She was afraid, so she immediately phoned the police and asked them to come to her house. When the police arrived, they found something very strange: the man who had broken into the house was asleep in one of the bedrooms!
>
> The thief had gone into Mrs Johnson's house, and had started to put some things into a big bag. But then he had found some food in the kitchen, and, because he was hungry, he had eaten it all. Feeling sleepy, he had gone into a bedroom, and he had fallen asleep!

b Match the sentences. Write a–h in the boxes.

1 I didn't watch the film on TV last night. `c`
2 I didn't recognise my cousin.
3 There weren't any books left in the shop.
4 I woke up very late yesterday.
5 My mum couldn't use the car.
6 I was pleased when I beat Sarah at tennis.
7 My sister had to go to hospital last week.
8 We really enjoyed our trip to New York.

a I hadn't switched my alarm clock on the night before.
b We hadn't been there before.
c I'd seen it three times before.
d They'd sold them all.
e She'd hurt herself in a volleyball match.
f He'd changed a lot since the last time I saw him.
g I'd never won a game against her before.
h Our dad had taken her keys with him.

Hello? Police?

c Complete the sentences with the past perfect form of the verbs in brackets.

1 When I switched on the TV, the programme _had finished_ (finish).

2 I couldn't pay because I _____ (leave) my money at home.

3 I didn't do very well in the test because I _____ (not study) the night before.

4 I went to France last year. It was the first time I _____ (visit) another country.

5 There wasn't any ice cream left because my brother and sister _____ (eat) it all.

6 The shop wouldn't change the shirt I'd bought because I _____ (lose) the receipt.

7 We couldn't buy a new USB stick because the shops _____ (shut).

8 You looked bored in the cinema. _____ you _____ (see) the film before?

d Complete the sentences with the past simple or past perfect form of the verbs in brackets.

1 When James _arrived_ (arrive) at the station, the train _had left_ (leave).

2 Our neighbour _____ (be) really angry with us because our ball _____ (break) his window.

3 I _____ (not buy) the shirt I wanted because I _____ (spend) all my money on CDs!

4 Jane _____ (not be) pleased when Alex came to her party, because she _____ (not invite) him.

5 I lost all my work because I _____ (forget) to save it before the electricity _____ (go) off!

6 I _____ (look) everywhere for my books, but I couldn't remember where I _____ (put) them.

e Complete the text with the past simple or past perfect form of the verbs in brackets.

In 1962, Nelson Mandela, the leader of the African National Congress (ANC), was sent to prison for life. The ANC _fought_ (fight) against the idea of apartheid, a system in South Africa which [1] _____ (not give) black people the same rights as white people. While Mandela [2] _____ (be) in prison, he [3] _____ (become) very famous all over the world.

The South African Government [4] _____ (allow) Mandela to leave prison in 1990 – he [5] _____ (be) a prisoner for more than 27 years. After leaving prison, he [6] _____ (continue) to work for the black people in his country. Mandela and the President, de Klerk, [7] _____ (win) the Nobel Peace Prize in 1993 because they [8] _____ (work) very hard for peace.

In 1994, Mandela [9] _____ (become) President of South Africa. There [10] _____ (not be) a black president before him.

2 Pronunciation

✱ had

a ▶ CD3 T32 Underline the word *had* where it is stressed. Circle the word *had* where it is weak.

1 I had a pizza last night.

2 It was the best pizza I had ever eaten.

3 My mum had a great idea.

4 It was the best idea my mum had ever had.

5 We had a holiday in Italy last year.

6 My family had always wanted to go there.

b ▶ CD3 T32 Listen, check and repeat.

3 Vocabulary

★ Noun suffixes: -r, -er, -or and -ist

a Look at pictures 1–10 and fill in the crossword.

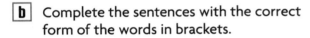

Crossword:
1 across: a r t i s t

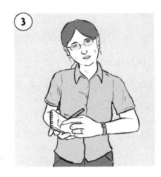

b Complete the sentences with the correct form of the words in brackets.

1 My brother's a really good _photographer_ . (photograph)

2 When I was young, I always wanted to be a famous _____ . (explore)

3 My sister always wanted to be a train _____ . (drive)

4 I'm sorry, I don't know this town – I'm just a _____ here. (tour)

5 I read in the paper that an _____ has found a new planet. (astronomy)

6 My mother works in a company in town – she's the _____ . (manage)

7 I'm sure it's really interesting to be a _____ and work for a newspaper. (journal)

8 My cousin works in a hotel – he's a _____ , but he hopes to be the manager one day! (reception)

9 My dad doesn't like doing things in the house, so we're getting a _____ to do my bedroom. (decorate)

10 I love old things, so when I leave school, I want to be an _____ . (archaeology)

4 Culture in mind

Complete the sentences with *El Dorado, Atlantis* or *Shambhala*. Then check with the text on page 100 of the Student's Book.

1 One story says that the gods decided to destroy ___*Atlantis*___ because its people had become greedy and wanted more power.

2 The legend of _____ began in 1537.

3 _____ is the name of a mystical kingdom behind the Himalayas.

4 The Spanish sent lots of people to look for _____ , but they never found it.

5 Some people say that _____ never existed, but was invented by Greek philosopher, Plato.

6 _____ was the name for a chief who covered himself in gold.

5 Study help

✱ Vocabulary: suffixes

a Suffixes are added to words to change the part of speech. Study the examples:

- Many suffixes, for example, *-ful, -less, -able*, change a noun or verb into an adjective. For example, *use: useful/useless/usable.*

- Other suffixes, for example, *-er, -ist, -ation*, change a verb into a noun. For example, *paint: painter; transform: transformation.*

b Underline the suffixes in these words. What part of speech is each one? Write *noun* or *adjective*.

1	art<u>ist</u>	*noun*	5 comfortable	_____
2	hopeful	_____	6 hopeless	_____
3	programmer	_____	7 lovable	_____
4	relaxation	_____	8 imagination	_____

c Add a suffix to each word in the box and write it in the correct column.

archaeology   art   climb   decorate   ~~explain~~   inform   paint
communicate   ~~science~~   swim   tour   combine   violin   ~~act~~

-ation	-ist	-er / -or
explanation	*scientist*	*actor*

6 Listen

▶ CD3 T33 Greg went to Machu Picchu last year with his father. He is talking to a friend about the trip. Listen and answer the questions. Tick (✓) the correct pictures.

1 What time did they take the train from Cuzco?

2 What was it like inside the train?

3 What had happened to the railway tracks?

4 What did Greg do after the train accident?

WRITING TIP

How to write a good narrative

Organisation

- At the start, give the background and include other important information. For example, where did the story happen? Who are the main characters?

- Start a new paragraph for each stage of the story. For example, *1 – the background to the story*; *2 – the main events*; and *3 – the ending*. Make sure your ending is interesting!

Language

- To make your story interesting, you need a variety of tenses: past simple, past continuous and past perfect. Be careful to choose the right one! Remember to use adjectives and adverbs to make the story more interesting.

- Always check your work when you have finished writing! In an examination, allow at least five minutes to do this.

7 Write

Write a short story about a journey where something went wrong.

Unit check

1 Fill in the spaces

Complete the text by adding the suffixes *-r*, *-er*, *-ist* or *-or* to the words in brackets.

I'd like to be a famous _footballer_ (football) like Cristiano Ronaldo, but my father thinks that I should be a [1]_____ (journal) with the local newspaper! My mother thinks it would be better if I became a [2]_____ (reception) because that's what she wanted to be! But if I worked in a hotel, I'd want to be the [3]_____ (own), of course! I don't want to have a job like my uncle – he's a [4]_____ (decorate) – or my cousin, who's a [5]_____ (teach) in London. Maybe I could be a [6]_____ (travel) and go round the world with a famous [7]_____ (explore). Or I could be a fantastic [8]_____ (art) like Picasso. But what I really want to be is a [9]_____ (cycle) and win the Tour de France!

| 9 |

2 Choose the correct answers

Circle the correct answer: a, b or c.

1 I wanted to see you, but you _____ to London.

a have gone   b (had gone)   c has gone

2 I _____ Julie for years until I saw her this morning.

a haven't seen   b did not see   c hadn't seen

3 The film _____ at four and finished at six.

a had start   b have started   c started

4 Dad was very happy when he saw that we _____ his car.

a had washed   b have washed   c washed

5 There _____ any tickets left.

a hadn't been   b weren't   c wasn't

6 I was really angry when I found out that they _____ you my secret.

a was telling   b tell   c had told

7 My dad couldn't drive to work yesterday because he _____ the car keys!

a has lost   b had lost   c was losing

8 I didn't see Jane because she had left before I _____ .

a 've arrived   b 'd arrived   c arrived

9 I couldn't give the teacher my homework because I _____ it at home.

a was leaving   b have left   c had left

| 8 |

3 Vocabulary

Put the letters in the correct order to find the verb or the adjective. Turn them into nouns.

1 lpmub   _____plumber_____

2 aetrlv   _____

3 oleeclt   _____

4 rfma   _____

5 ggujle   _____

6 lhgaieoralcca   _____

7 rtenesp   _____

8 nnetiv   _____

9 iwn   _____

| 8 |

How did you do?

Total: | 25 |

| :) Very good 20 – 25 | :| OK 14 – 19 | :(Review Unit 13 again 0 – 13 |

14 A stroke of luck

1 Remember and check

a Complete the summary of the story using words in the box. Change the form if necessary. Then check with the text on page 102 of the Student's Book.

> buy ~~have~~ land act broken come off go fall out fly

French art teacher Pierre Chevalier is probably the world's luckiest man. About 40 years ago, he _had_ his first accident when he was on a train ride. The train [1]_____ the tracks and fell into an icy river. Twelve passengers were killed, but Chevalier survived and had only a [2]_____ leg and shock.

Two years later, he was on a plane when a door suddenly opened and he [3]_____ . Soon after that, the plane crashed and lots of passengers were killed. Again Chevalier survived, this time because he [4]_____ in a haystack. After surviving many accidents, he [5]_____ his first lottery ticket ever and won!

After this, an American TV company invited Chevalier to [6]_____ in an advertisement. But he didn't want to [7]_____ again. If Chevalier [8]_____ to America, he might have had another accident!

b Match the two parts of the sentences. Then check with the text on page 102 of the Student's Book.

1 If Chevalier hadn't been on the train,
2 If he hadn't landed in a haystack,
3 He would have been killed in a car accident
4 If he hadn't won the lottery,
5 If he had flown to Los Angeles,
6 If he'd had another accident,

a if he hadn't jumped out of the car.
b he probably would have survived that one too!
c he might have had another accident.
d he wouldn't have broken his leg.
e he wouldn't have bought a car, a house and a speedboat.
f his injuries would have been far worse.

2 Grammar

✳ Reported statements

a Complete the table. Write the grammar descriptions and the example sentences.

DIRECT SPEECH	REPORTED SPEECH
Present simple	**Past simple**
I'm a writer.	She said she was a writer.
Present _continuous_	**Past** _continuous_
I'm writing a book about a ghost.	She said she _was writing_ a book about a ghost.
Present _____	_____
They've never been to London.	They said they _____ to London.
Past simple	_____
We arrived last week.	They said they _____ the week before.
am/is/are going to	_____ **going to**
My uncle's going to live in Paris.	He said his uncle _____ in Paris.
can/can't	_____ / _____
I can't come on Saturday.	She said she _____ on Saturday.
will/won't	_____ / _____
I'll go next week.	He said he _____ the following week.

b Read the dialogue. Then complete the paragraph using reported speech.

Woman: Excuse me. I need some help.

Me: Oh, OK. I'll be happy to help you.

Woman: I've never been here before, and someone stole my purse this morning.

Me: Well, I'm sorry. I haven't got any money.

Woman: No, that's OK – I don't want money. I'm trying to find the police station.

Me: Oh, I see. Well, I'm going that way, so I can take you there.

Woman: Great – thank you very much.

Yesterday a woman came up to me in town. She looked worried and said she _needed_ some help. I felt sorry for her, so I said I [1] _____ happy to help her. She told me she [2] _____ to the town before, and she said that someone [3] _____ her purse that morning. I said I [4] _____ sorry but I [5] _____ any money. The woman said she [6] _____ money – she said she [7] _____ to find the police station. So I told her that I [8] _____ that way, and I said I [9] _____ her there. She was very pleased!

c ▶ CD3 T34 Sandra, Claudia, Josh and Mitsuko are talking about an amusement park. Listen to what they said about the park. Who likes it? Who doesn't like it?

----

d ▶ CD3 T34 Listen again. Complete the summaries. Use reported speech.

Sandra and Claudia, from Italy

Sandra and Claudia said they _had arrived_ there at [1] _____ . They said that some of the rides [2] _____ , but they also said the queues [3] _____ and they [4] _____ it [5] _____ very expensive there.

Josh, from Britain

Josh told me he thought it [6] _____ place. He said all the rides [7] _____ , but his [8] _____ *The Elevator*. He said [9] _____ three times and that he [10] _____ again.

Mitsuko, from Japan

Mitsuko said that she [11] _____ the park very much. She said that [12] _____ very scary, and she said she [13] _____ them. She also told me that she [14] _____ there again.

3 Vocabulary

✱ Noun suffixes, with *-ation* and *-ment*

a Find and (circle) the noun forms of the verbs in the box.

calculate	cancel	invite	equip
~~improve~~	inform	manage	

L	E	E	I	M	P	R	O	V	E	M	E	N	T
S	D	Q	N	A	E	Q	I	I	N	P	M	T	Z
C	U	U	F	N	R	S	N	J	T	E	R	I	E
A	C	I	O	G	F	A	V	Q	E	E	P	M	N
L	A	P	R	A	O	L	I	U	R	X	F	A	T
C	U	M	M	G	N	I	T	A	T	I	O	N	E
U	F	E	A	T	R	V	A	S	P	N	G	A	R
L	G	N	T	I	E	N	T	E	I	R	A	G	E
A	N	T	I	O	N	O	I	O	N	T	R	E	D
T	B	C	O	M	M	U	O	A	M	R	E	M	N
I	O	R	N	K	P	O	N	E	E	M	E	E	D
O	C	A	N	C	E	L	L	A	T	I	O	N	E
N	I	N	F	C	A	L	C	U	T	I	N	T	O

b Rewrite the sentences, using the nouns from the grid in Exercise 3a.

1 We sold our house after we had improved it a lot.
We sold our house after we had made a lot of *improvement*s to it.

2 My cousin invited us to her birthday party. We got an .... to my cousin's birthday party.

3 The people here don't manage things very well.
The .... here isn't very good.

4 They informed us about a lot of things. They gave us a lot of ....

5 We calculated how much money we needed to spend. We made a .... to see how much money we needed to spend.

6 There weren't any ticket ....s, so we couldn't go to the football match.

7 We're going to the mountains for a few days, so we'll need some camping ....

4 Vocabulary bank

Complete the sentences with the words in the box.

pot luck	superstitious	all the luck
touch wood	by chance	
fingers crossed	~~good luck~~	bad luck

1 Some people say that a horse shoe can bring you *good luck* .

2 We had no idea which book would be more interesting, so we just took .... and selected one that had a nice cover.

3 I've got my maths test tomorrow – please keep your .... for me.

4 A: I found a lottery ticket on the ground, and I won!
   B: Really? Well, some people have .... !

5 I hadn't heard of the film before. I saw it .... on TV, and it was brilliant!

6 A: Tomorrow is Friday the 13th and it's my birthday. That'll bring me .... !
   B: Don't be .... ! It might bring you good luck!

7 Peter's promised to be here at 8.30 tomorrow – so we'll start at nine o'clock, ...

5 Grammar

✳ Third conditional

For each pair of sentences, write one sentence in the third conditional.

1 Alex was late for school. The teacher was angry with him.

   If Alex hadn't been late for school, the
   teacher wouldn't have been angry with him.

2 Alex didn't listen to the questions. He got all the answers wrong.

   If Alex had listened _____
   _____ .

3 He got all the answers wrong. The other kids laughed at him.

   If he hadn't _____
   _____ .

4 The other kids laughed at him. He felt really miserable.

   He wouldn't _____
   _____ .

5 He felt really miserable. He ate a huge lunch.

   _____
   _____
   _____ .

6 He ate a huge lunch. He was sick later on.

   _____
   _____
   _____ .

6 Pronunciation

✳ *would ('d) have / wouldn't have*

a ▶ **CD3 T35** Listen and repeat.

1 I'd have gone.
2 She'd have told you.
3 They wouldn't have done it.
4 We'd have eaten before.

b ▶ **CD3 T36** Listen and repeat.

1 I'd have gone to the party if I hadn't been ill.
2 She'd have told you if she'd known.
3 They wouldn't have done it if you'd been there.
4 We'd have eaten before if we'd been hungry.

7 Everyday English

Complete the dialogues. Use the expressions in the box.

> it's a bit like   surely   what's going on
> was like   ~~have a word~~   it's just that

A **Sally:** Louise? Can I ___*have a word*___ with you?

   Louise: Of course, Sally. Why? Is something wrong?

   Sally: No, not really.

   ¹ _____ I want to talk to someone about Patrick.

   Louise: You mean, your boyfriend Patrick? OK, so tell me –

   ² _____ ?

B **Jamie:** I had an argument with my dad last night. I broke a plate and he

   ³ _____ 'Why can't you be more careful?', you know?

   Oliver: Yeah, I know!

   ⁴ _____ when I lost my mum's camera. She really shouted at me!

   Jamie: What's the matter with our parents? ⁵ _____ they had accidents when they were teenagers, too?

Skills in mind

8 Study help

✱ How to revise

Read these tips to help you to revise for your exams:

- Look again at your scores in the *Check your progress* sections of the Student's Book. Which areas of grammar or vocabulary did you do well in? Which areas did you do less well in?

- For the things that you didn't do well in, read the examples, rules and exercises in the Student's Book again carefully. Do the same with the *Unit checks* in this Workbook.

- Check through your Workbook. Are there any exercises that you haven't done yet? Do them now!

- It is also a good idea to repeat some exercises that you did well before.

9 Read

a Read this letter to the newspaper. Did the writer enjoy the film?

b Write *T* (true), *F* (false) or *N* (not in the text).

1. Philip Lawrence wrote a review of the film *Slumdog Millionaire*. [T]

2. James disagrees with everything Philip Lawrence said. [ ]

3. James saw the film last week. [ ]

4. James thought that the acting was good but the directing wasn't. [ ]

5. James thinks that the film director didn't choose the right actor. [ ]

6. Lawrence thinks that American films are better than films made in foreign countries. [ ]

7. James didn't like the last Hollywood film he saw. [ ]

8. James thinks that cinema tickets are too expensive. [ ]

Dear Sir or Madam,

Last week I read Philip Lawrence's review of the film *Slumdog Millionaire* and I am writing to say that, in my view, Mr Lawrence was wrong in everything he said.

1 _____ , he said that the film was not good enough to be nominated for Oscars, 2 _____ I thought the film was an excellent production, with very high quality acting and directing, and I enjoyed it enormously.

3 _____ , Mr Lawrence said that the young actor Dev Patel was not a good choice 4 _____ he 'was not an experienced actor'. Personally, 5 _____ that Patel gave an excellent performance, even though he hasn't had much acting experience. The film would not have been better if the director had chosen a trained teenage actor.

6 _____ , Mr Lawrence said that films made in foreign countries are not as good as films from the USA. Hasn't he seen some of the awful films that come out of Hollywood? 7 _____ , the money for a cinema ticket is much better spent on films like *Slumdog Millionaire*.

Yours,

James Singleton

WRITING TIP

Revision

In other units in this Workbook, you have seen ideas to help you with your writing. These include:

- making your writing more interesting (Unit 2)
- using linkers like *first of all, secondly*, etc. (Unit 3)
- writing informal letters and emails (Unit 5)
- using linkers like *then, finally*, etc. (Unit 9)
- how to write a good narrative (Unit 13)

Complete the letter in Exercise 9a with the words in the box.

> but   secondly   I think   first of all
> in my opinion   ~~dear~~   because   finally

Unit check

1 Fill in the spaces

Complete the text with nouns made from the verbs in the box.

educate   equip   improve   calculate   manage   entertain   communicate   ~~inform~~

Yesterday, the people at Millers & Co got some _information_ from the company's ¹_____ . They said the new office ²_____ should not be used for watching DVDs or any other kind of ³_____ . They said that the recent ⁴_____s to the computer system were intended to provide better ⁵_____ between the company and the customers. The manager had done some ⁶_____s, and they show that watching DVDs during office hours will cost the company over £25,000 per year. Millers & Co plan to introduce training courses which will lead to better ⁷_____ for the employees. | 7 |

2 Choose the correct answers

Circle the correct answer: a, b or c.

1   Mum told me that she _____ me to help.
    a (wanted)   b wanting   c want

2   I asked them where they _____ for their next holiday.
    a were going   b had gone   c go

3   Jane told me she _____ drive me to school.
    a could   b has   c could be

4   She asked me if we _____ hungry.
    a have   b was   c were

5   We asked her what she _____ us to do.
    a has wanted   b want   c wanted

6   I asked Tom why he _____ his promise.
    a had forgotten   b forget   c forgets

7   He asked her if she _____ to Italy.
    a had been   b was   c been

8   They would have invited you if _____ you.
    a they saw   b they've seen   c they'd seen

9   If I'd known the answer, I _____ you.
    a would have told   b had told   c would tell

10 If Kate _____ a lot of homework, we could have gone out together.
    a hadn't had   b hadn't   c wouldn't have

| 9 |

3 Vocabulary

Complete the sentences with nouns made from the verbs in the box.

~~improve~~   treat   react   accommodate   pay
cancel   invite   reserve   calculate   inform

1   The new DVD player wasn't an _improvement_ . The old one was better.

2   That restaurant is always full. I think we should make a _____ .

3   Sorry, but we only accept _____ by credit card.

4   I'm not going to her party – I didn't get an _____ .

5   You lost her DVD? What was her _____ when you told her?

6   I didn't like staying in that tent. Next time, I want better _____ !

7   The hotel's full. We'll only get a room if there's a _____ .

8   Can you give us some _____ about the city?

9   Scientists have discovered a new _____ for this illness.

10 I've done a quick _____ and it's clear we need more money!

| 9 |

How did you do?

Total: | 25 |

| 😊 | Very good 20 – 25 | 😐 | OK 14 – 19 | 🙁 | Review Unit 14 again 0 – 13 |

Grammar reference

Unit 1

Past continuous

1   We use the past continuous to talk about actions in progress at a certain time in the past.
    *In 1999, we **were living** in the USA.   The television was on, but I **wasn't watching** it.*

2   The past continuous is formed with the past simple of *be* + verb + *ing*.
    *You **were running** very fast.*   *You **weren't running** very fast.*
    *Andy **was listening** to the radio.*   *Andy **wasn't watching** television.*

3   The question is formed with the past simple of *be* + subject + verb + *ing*.
    ***Was** James **running**?*   *Yes, he **was**. ╱ No, he **wasn't**.*
    ***Were** your parents **having** lunch?*   *Yes, they **were**. ╱ No, they **weren't**.*
    *What **were** you **studying**?*
    *Why **was** she **crying**?*

Past continuous vs. past simple

1   When we talk about the past, we use the past simple for actions that happened at one particular time.
    We use the past continuous for background actions.
    *When my friend **arrived**, I **was having** lunch.   He **was cycling** very fast and he **had** an accident.*
    *What **did** you **say**? I **wasn't listening**.*

2   We often use *when* with the past simple, and *while* with the past continuous.
    *I was sleeping **when** the phone rang.   **While** Jack was washing the dishes, he dropped a plate.*

Unit 2

Comparative and superlative adjectives

1   When we want to compare two things, or two groups of things, we use a comparative form + *than*.
    *I'm **taller than** my father.*
    *DVDs are **more expensive than** CDs.*
    *His watch is **better than** mine.*

2   With short adjectives, we normally add *er*.
    *cold – cold**er**   long – long**er**   clever – clever**er***

    If the adjective ends in *e*, we add only *r*.
    *white – white**r**   safe – safe**r***

    If the adjective ends with consonant + *y*, we change the *y* to *i* and add *er*.
    *easy – eas**ier**   early – earl**ier**   happy – happ**ier***

    If the adjective ends in one vowel + one consonant, we double the final consonant and add *er*.
    *big – big**ger**   fat – fat**ter**   slim – slim**mer***

3   With longer adjectives (more than two syllables), we don't change the adjective – we put *more* in front of it.
    *expensive – **more** expensive   boring – **more** boring*

4   Some adjectives have a different comparative form.
    *good – **better**   bad – **worse**   far – **further***

5   We can modify the comparison, by using *much/far*, *a lot* or *a little ╱ a bit*. These words come before
    the normal comparison.
    *This film is **much** better than the book.*
    *His pronunciation is **far** worse than mine.*
    *We walked **a bit** further than last week.*

Adverbs

1 We use adverbs to describe verbs – they say how an action is or was performed.
   She <u>smiled</u> **happily**.   <u>Drive</u> **slowly**!
   We <u>got</u> to school **late**.

   We can also use adverbs before adjectives.
   It was **bitterly** <u>cold</u> yesterday.   The sea was **beautifully** <u>warm</u>, so we went swimming.

2 Most adverbs are formed by adjective + ly.
   quiet – quiet**ly**   bad – bad**ly**

   If the adjective ends in le, we drop the e and add y.
   terrible – terrib**ly**   comfortable – comfortab**ly**

   If the adjective ends in consonant + y, we change the y to i and add ly.
   easy – eas**ily**   happy – happ**ily**   lucky – luck**ily**

3 Some adverbs are irregular – they don't have an ly ending.
   good – **well**   fast – **fast**   hard – **hard**   early – **early**   late – **late**

Comparison of adverbs

1 To compare adverbs, we use the same rules as we do when we compare adjectives. With short adverbs, we add er or r, and than after the adverb.
   I was late for school, but my brother was **later than** me!

2 With longer adverbs, we use more (adverb) + than.
   I ran **more quickly** than the others.

3 To compare the adverb well, we use better ... than. To compare the adverb far, we use further ... than.
   Steve plays tennis **better than** me.   My school is **further** from my house **than** the park.

Unit 3

will/won't, or might/may (not) for prediction

1 We can use the modal verb will ('ll) or will not (won't) to make predictions about the future.
   Don't worry about the exam next week – it **won't be** difficult.

2 We use might/might not (mightn't) or may/may not to make less certain predictions about the future.
   I'm not sure, but I think I **might go** to university when I leave school.

3 Like all modal verbs, will/won't and might/might not and may/may not are followed by the base form of the main verb, and the form is the same for all subjects.
   I think it'll **be** a nice day tomorrow. (**NOT** ~~I think it'll to be a nice day tomorrow.~~)
   My brother might go to live in the USA. (**NOT** ~~My brother might to go to live in the USA.~~)
   She may not pass her driving test.

4 We make questions with will by putting the subject **after** the modal verb.
   Will we **have** a test next week?

First conditional

1 We often make conditional sentences by using If + subject + present simple in the if clause, and will/won't / might/might not in the main clause.
   If we have time, **we'll do** some shopping at the supermarket.
   I might go out tonight **if there's** nothing good on TV.

2 We can also use the word unless in conditional sentences – it means if ... not.
   Unless the teacher explains, we won't know what to do. (= **If** the teacher **doesn't** explain, we won't know what to do.)
   James won't know **unless** you tell him. (= James won't know **if** you **don't** tell him.)

3 There are two clauses in these sentences. We can put the main clause first, or the if/unless clause first. When the if/unless clause comes first, there is a comma after it.
   Unless the teacher explains, we won't know what to do.
   We won't know what to do unless the teacher explains.

Unit 4

Question tags

1 Question tags are positive or negative questions at the end of statements. We add 'tags' to the end of statements:

   a) when **we are not sure** that what we are saying is correct, and we want the other person to say if we are correct or not.

   b) when **we are sure** that what we are saying is correct, and we want the other person to say something about it.

2 Tags in (a) above have a rising intonation pattern.

   *A: You're French, **aren't you**?*   *B: No, I'm not. I'm Swiss.*

   Tags in (b) above have a falling intonation pattern.

   *A: You're French, **aren't you**?*   *B: That's right. I'm from Marseilles.*

3 With **positive** statements, we usually use a **negative** question tag.

   *I'm late, **aren't I**?*   *He's lazy, **isn't he**?*

   With **negative** statements, we usually use a **positive** question tag.

   *I'm not late, **am I**?*   *He isn't lazy, **is he**?*

Present perfect

1 We use the present perfect (present tense of *have* + past participle) to talk about a present situation, and the events in the past that are connected to the present situation.

   *The teacher's angry because we **haven't done** our homework.*   *I've eaten too much food, and I **feel** ill.*

2 There is an important difference between *have gone* and *have been*.

   *My friend Sarah **has been** to Cuba on holiday. (= Sarah went to Cuba, and she has come back again.)*

   *My friend Sarah **has gone** to Cuba on holiday. (= Sarah went to Cuba, and she is still there.)*

Present perfect + *already/yet/just*

1 We often use the words *already* and *yet* with the present perfect. We use *already* in positive sentences, and *yet* in negative sentences and in questions.

   The word *already* usually comes between *have* and the past participle. The word *yet* usually comes at the end of the sentence or question.

   *I don't want to watch the film on TV tonight – I've **already seen** it.*

   *I started this work two hours ago, but I **haven't finished** it **yet**.*

2 When we use the word *just* with the present perfect, it means 'not very long ago'. Like *already*, it is usually placed between *have* and the past participle.

   *I've **just heard** that my favourite band has released a new CD – great!*

   *Do you want a piece of cake? My mother's **just made** it.*

Unit 5

Present simple passive

1 We use the passive when it isn't important who does the action, or when we don't know who does it.

   *These watches **are made** in Switzerland. (We don't know who makes them.)*

   *Jeans **are made** of denim. (It isn't important who makes them.)*

2 To form the present simple passive, we use the present simple tense of the verb *to be* + the past participle of the main verb.

   *Football **is played** in many countries.*   *The animals in the zoo **are fed** every morning.*

let and *be allowed to*

1 We use *be allowed to* to say that you do (or don't) have permission to do something.

   *At my school, we **are allowed to** wear jeans.*   *You **aren't allowed to** smoke in restaurants in New York.*

2 We use *let* to say that someone gives you, or doesn't give you, permission to do something.

   *I **let** my brother borrow my bicycle sometimes.*   *Our teacher **didn't let** us use dictionaries in the test.*

3 Both *let* and *be allowed to* are followed by the infinitive.

   *I'm not allowed to **watch** the late-night film.*   *My dad didn't let me **watch** the late-night film.*

4 With *let*, the structure is *let* + person + bare infinitive (without *to*).

   *She **didn't let me answer** the question.*   *I'm not going to **let you borrow** my CD player.*

Unit 6

Present perfect with *for* and *since*

1   We can use the present perfect to talk about something that began in the past and continues to be true in the present.
    *I **have lived** here for ten years. (= I started living here ten years ago, and I still live here.)*

2   We talk about the time between when something started and now with *for* or *since*.

    We use the word *for* when we mention **a period of time** from the past until now.
    *for **an hour**   for **two years**   for **a long time***

    We use the word *since* when we mention a **point in time** in the past.
    *since **ten o'clock**   since **1992**   since **last Saturday***

Unit 7

Past simple passive

1   We form the past simple passive with the past simple of the verb *to be* and the past participle of the main verb.
    *The car **was destroyed** in the accident, and two people **were injured**.*

2   We use the passive when it isn't important who does the action, or when we don't know who does it (see Unit 6).

3   Sometimes when we use the passive (present or past), we want to say who or what did the action.
    To do this, we use the word *by* + noun.
    *A lot of mistakes <u>are made</u> **by students**.   He <u>was arrested</u> **by the police**.*

a(n) and *the*

1   We use *a* or *an* (the indefinite articles) when we are talking about something for the **first** time.
    *I gave my sister **a** DVD for her birthday.   I usually eat **an** apple for breakfast.*

    We also use *a/an* with a noun when we are talking about something in general, and not a special example of something.
    *I think it's nicer to live in **a** house than in **a** flat.   Let's go and have **an** ice cream.*

2   We use *the* (the definite article) with a noun when it is clear which thing or person we are talking about. Sometimes this is when we talk about something for the **second** time.
    *I took a photograph of my sister, but **the** photograph was awful!*

    Sometimes it is because there is only one of the thing we are talking about.
    ***The** sun is really hot today. (= There is only one sun.)*

    Sometimes it is because the person we are talking to already knows which thing we mean.
    *Can I use **the** computer now? (= The listener knows which computer you are talking about.)*

3   We also use *the* when we talk about certain things in general, for example, *the cinema, the telephone, the internet.*
    *I really like going to **the** cinema. (= the cinema as a general place, not a particular cinema)*

Unit 8

too many/much, not enough

1   *too many* and *too much* are phrases that we use to say that there is more of something than is wanted.
    *I've got **too many** CDs. (= I don't have a place to put all the CDs that I've got.)*

2   We use *too many* before plural countable nouns.
    *There are **too many cars** on the streets.   I think we get **too many tests**.*

3   We use *too much* before uncountable nouns.
    *Don't put **too much water** on the plants.   Don't spend **too much money** in that shop.*

4   *not enough* is the opposite of *too much / too many*. We use this phrase to say that more is needed.
    *There aren't **enough** people here to play a football match. (= We need more people.)*

5   *not enough* is used with plural countable nouns, or with uncountable nouns. We put *not* with the verb, and *enough* before the noun.

will vs. *be going to*

1 We can use *be going to* or *will* to talk about the future, but there is some difference in the meanings that they have.

2 We use *be going to* when we talk about something in the future which is a result of what we can see now, or that we know now.
   *Look at those black clouds in the sky! It's **going to** rain.*

3 We use *be going to* when we talk about our (or other people's) intentions and plans for the future.
   *We're **going to play** volleyball this afternoon. (= We've already decided to do this.)*

4 We often use will when we decide to do something at the moment of speaking.
   *I'm bored – I think I'll **go** for a walk.*

Unit 9

everyone / no one, etc.

1 We can use the words *every/some/no* together with *one/thing/where* to make compound nouns.

2 These words mean:

everyone = *all the people*	someone = *a person, but we don't know who*	no one = *none of the people*
everything = *all the things*	something = *a thing, but we don't know which*	nothing = *none of the things*
everywhere = *all the places*	somewhere = *a place, but we don't know where*	nowhere = *none of the places*

3 These words are all singular.
   ***Something's** wrong.   No one's perfect.   Nothing **was** found.   Everywhere **was** full.   Someone **has** taken my pen.*

4 We don't use negatives with *nothing* and *no one*. We use *anything* or *anyone* instead.
   *I **don't know anyone** here.* (**NOT** ~~I don't know no one here.~~)

5 With other nouns and pronouns, we use *all of / some of / none of* + plural or uncountable noun/pronoun.
   ***All of** the CDs are mine.   **Some of** the teachers are really nice.   **None of** my friends came to my party.*

must/mustn't vs. *don't have to*

1 *mustn't* is the negative of *must*. We use *mustn't* to say that something is the wrong thing to do, or when we give someone an obligation **not** to do something.
   *Teacher: Be quiet! You **mustn't talk** in the lessons!*

2 *don't/doesn't have to* is the negative of *have to*. We use *don't/doesn't have to* to say that something is not necessary.
   *I love Sundays because I **don't have to get up** early.*

Unit 10

Present perfect continuous

1 The present perfect continuous is formed with the present tense of *have + been +* the *ing* form of the verb.
   *I've **been waiting** for two hours.   It's **been raining** since last weekend.*

2 Sentences with the present perfect always connect the present and the past. We often use the present perfect continuous to talk about situations which started in the past and are still continuing now.
   *I've **been waiting** for two hours.   (= I started waiting two hours ago, and I am still waiting.)*

3 We also use the present perfect continuous to talk about actions with a result in the present. These actions may or may not be complete.
   *I'm **tired** because I've **been working** hard.*

4 We also use the present perfect continuous to talk about actions which began in the past and continue to the present, but perhaps we are not doing the action at the time of speaking.
   *I've **been learning** English for two years.   (= I started learning two years ago, and I am still learning, but I'm not learning at this moment.)*

Present perfect simple and present perfect continuous

1 We use the present perfect simple to show that an action is finished, or to focus on what we have completed in a period of time.
   *I've **written** a letter.   I've **written** three letters this morning.*

2 We use the present perfect continuous to show that an action is still going on, or to focus on how long something has been in progress.

I've been reading this book for two hours.   *I've been reading detective stories for years.*

3 There are some verbs which cannot usually be used in the continuous. These verbs often express a permanent state. For example, *know, understand, have* (for possession), *like, hate*. For these verbs we use the present perfect simple (see also Unit 1 present simple and present continuous).

She's known her teacher since she was in the first class. (**NOT** ~~She's been knowing ...~~)

Unit 11

Defining relative clauses

1 A defining relative clause is something we use to say exactly who or what we are talking about.

*The boy was friendly. The boy **who told me that joke** was friendly.*

2 To make these clauses, we use these words: *who/which/that/where*. We use *who* or *that* for people. We use *which* or *that* for things and animals. We use *where* for places.

*That's the man **who** told me. OR That's the man **that** told me.*

used to

1 We can use the expression *used to* when we want to talk about an action which happened regularly in the past, but which doesn't happen any more.

*My father **used to** smoke. (= My father smoked in the past, but he doesn't smoke any more.)*

2 *used to* is followed by the base form of the main verb.

*Our town **used to be** much smaller than it is now.*

3 The negative of *used to* is *didn't use to*.

*I **didn't use to** eat vegetables. (= In the past I didn't eat vegetables, but now I eat them.)*

We make questions with *used to* using *Did* + subject + *use to ...?*

*Did you **use to live** in London?*

The negative of *used to* and questions with *used to* are not written or said very often.

4 For actions that happened only once in the past, use the past simple.

*I **got married** last year.* (**NOT** ~~I used to get married ...~~)

Unit 12

Second conditional

1 We use the second conditional to talk about unreal or imagined situations in the present or future.

*If I **was a film star**, I **would live** in a house in Hollywood. (= I am <u>not</u> a film star, and I <u>don't live</u> in a house in Hollywood.)*

*Your parents **wouldn't look after** you if they didn't love you. (= Your parents <u>do</u> look after you, because they <u>do</u> love you.)*

2 The second conditional has two parts (or 'clauses'). We usually make the second conditional like this:

If clause	Main clause
If + past simple	*would/wouldn't* + main verb
*If my brother **had** more time,*	*he'd **help** me with my homework.*
*If Jenny **was** older,*	*she'd **leave** school and **get** a job.*

We can change the order of the two clauses if we want to.

*My brother **would help** me with my homework if he **had** more time.*

When we put the *if* clause first, we write a comma (,) after it. If we put the main clause first, there is no comma.

3 The word *would* is often spoken as *'d*. We can write it like this in informal writing, too. Also **would not** is often spoken as **wouldn't**.

4 When we use the verb *to be* in the *if* clause of second conditional sentences, we often use *were* for all persons, including *I* and *he/she/it*. This is especially true in the phrase *If I were you ...*

*If I **were** older, I'd live in my own flat. (OR If I **was** older, ...)*

Unit 13

Past perfect

1   We use the past perfect when we need to make it clear that one action happened **before** another action in the past.
*When I <u>arrived</u> at Jim's house, the party **had started**. (= The party started **before** I arrived.)*

Compare this with:
*When I <u>arrived</u> at Jim's house, the party **started**. (= I arrived, and **then** the party started.)*

2   We form the past perfect with *had/hadn't (had not)* + the past participle of the main verb.
*I didn't see Jane because she **had gone** out.*

3   When we use words like *before* and *after* in the past, it is often not necessary to use the past perfect, because *before* and *after* make it clear which action happened first.
*The party <u>started</u> before I <u>arrived</u>.   We <u>got</u> to the train station **after** the train <u>left</u>.*

4   We often use the words *already* and *just* with the past perfect – they go between *had* and the main verb.
*I didn't go to the cinema with them because I'<u>d</u> **already** <u>seen</u> the film.*

Unit 14

Reported statements

1   When we report what someone said in the past, we use reported speech. In reported speech, we use the verb *said* or *told (me)*, and change some of the things that the person actually said.
*'I'<u>m</u> hungry,' my sister said. → My sister **said she was** hungry.*

2   We can use the word *that* between *said* or *told (me)* and the rest of the sentence, or we can leave it out.
*I said **that** I didn't want a hamburger. OR I said I didn't want a hamburger.*

3   We often change the verb tense between direct speech and reported speech, like this:

Direct speech		Reported speech
Present (simple/continuous)	→	Past (simple/continuous)
Past (simple/continuous)	→	Past perfect (simple/continuous)
Present perfect	→	Past perfect
am/is/are going to	→	*was/were going to*
can/can't	→	*could/couldn't*
will/won't	→	*would/wouldn't*

Third conditional

1   We use the third conditional to talk about unreal, imaginary situations in the past.
If you had told the teacher, she wouldn't have been angry. (= You <u>didn't tell</u> the teacher, and she <u>was</u> angry.)

2   The third conditional has two parts (or clauses). We usually make the third conditional like this:

If clause	Main clause
If + past perfect	*would have / wouldn't have* + main verb
*If my brother **had told** me,*	*I'**d have known**.*
*If the team **hadn't played** so badly,*	*they **wouldn't have lost**.*

3   We can change the order of the two clauses if we want to.
*I **would have known** if my brother **had told** me.*
*The team **wouldn't have lost** if they **hadn't played** so badly.*

4   When we put the *if* clause first, we write a comma (,) after it. When we put the main clause first, there is no comma.